AVID

READER

PRESS

CALL! 774-325-0503

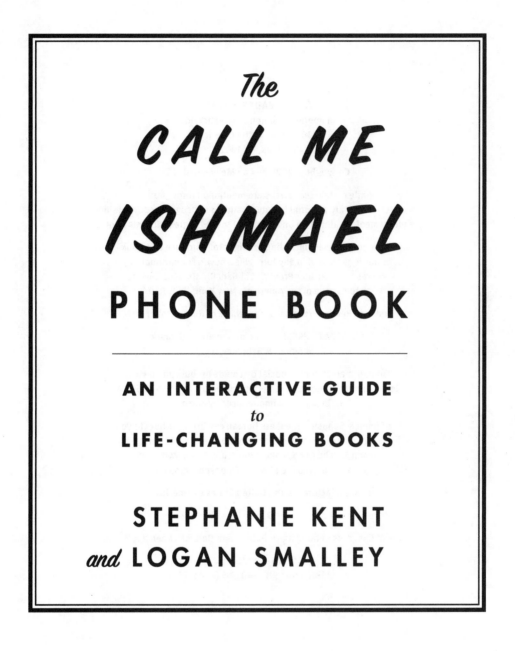

The CALL ME ISHMAEL PHONE BOOK

AN INTERACTIVE GUIDE *to* LIFE-CHANGING BOOKS

STEPHANIE KENT
and LOGAN SMALLEY

Avid Reader Press
New York London Toronto Sydney New Delhi

Avid Reader Press
An Imprint of Simon & Schuster, Inc.
1230 Avenue of the Americas
New York, NY 10020

While certain real places are mentioned throughout, these references are editorial in nature, and do not suggest sponsorship, endorsement, or affiliation on the part of these entities with this book.

First Avid Reader Press trade paperback edition October 2020

Manufactured in the United States of America

1 3 5 7 9 10 8 6 4 2

Library of Congress Cataloging-in-Publication Data has been applied for.

ISBN 978-1-9821-4058-8
ISBN 978-1-9821-4059-5 (ebook)

To Terrie and Barbara,
for making readers of us

CONTENTS

The CALL ME ISHMAEL PHONE BOOK

INTRODUCTION

One summer evening in Greenwich Village, we found ourselves at a pub debating the best opening lines in literature. One of us argued for Orwell's "It was a bright day in April and the clocks were striking thirteen" while the other championed Vonegut's "All this happened more or less." Unable to agree, we struck a truce over our shared appreciation for Melville's renowned opener: "Call Me Ishmael." We also, for the first time, spotted the pun. What would happen if booklovers could actually call *Moby-Dick*'s narrator and leave a voice message? Hours later, we'd created a working phone number and issued this challenge to readers everywhere: Tell us a story about a book you love. The messages started pouring in. We shared our favorites online, word continued to spread, and we've since amassed thousands of anonymous voicemail messages from bibliophiles all over the world. Receiving and listening to those messages has become an enduring source of joy in our lives. We're grateful and delighted to share that collection with you here, in the form of this Phone Book.

If you've seen a telephone directory before, *The Call Me Ishmael Phone Book* might feel familiar. Nostalgic, even. It may remind you of a slower time. You might once have dog-eared the pages of a book like this, circled your favorite local restaurants, underlined the phone number of a crosstown crush, or leveraged its thickness to sit a little taller at family dinner.

Maybe you've never seen a phone book, and you've always been able to reach your loved ones with the touch of a screen. For you, this book will help you discover stories from strangers in a way you never knew was possible. By the time you reach the end of their stories the wide and wired world might feel a little cozier, and a little more human.

Whether you miss your local Yellow Pages or you appreciate innovative ways to connect with people's stories, the book you're holding is an entirely new (and totally quirky) way to discover, explore, and celebrate life-changing books.

How to use this book to discover your next great read

Step 1 Call 774-325-0503 from any phone.

Step 2 Enter any four-digit extension that you find in this book.

Step 3 Listen to an anonymous reader share a story about a book they love.

Thousands of readers from around the world have left us voice messages about their most beloved books. Each message offers an answer to that age-old readers' conundrum: What should I read next? Follow the steps above to hear the calls for yourself, or read the transcripts of a few of our favorites (marked by the symbol ☎). You can browse the messages on the yellow pages by topic, or head to the white pages to view the listings in alphabetical order by author or book title.

How to use this book to explore bookish places

Step 1 Browse the yellow pages of this Phone Book and keep an eye out for this symbol📌, which demarks a real-life literary location that you can explore.

Step 2 Call 774-325-0503 and enter the associated four-digit extension to learn about the location.

Step 3 Visit the bookish destination in person or online. Be sure to tag us in your travels on Twitter and Instagram: @callingishmael.

Like the phone books of old, the *Call Me Ishmael Phone Book* can help you discover incredible, real-life locations. We have an affinity for bookstores, libraries, and literary tourism, which is why you'll find the real addresses of some of our favorite literary establishments throughout this book. Dial any location's four-digit extension to learn more about the adventure that awaits. Also, you'll find many independent bookstores tucked into various categories within the yellow pages of this book. Indie bookshops are some of our favorite places on earth, and while we couldn't possibly list every shop, we do hope you'll find and visit your local indie, and, if you're able, buy lots of books while you're there.

How to use this book to uncover literary surprises

Step 1 Read the Phone Book for listings, transcripts, and bookish places.

Step 2 Look for mysterious advertisements or puzzling pages.

Step 3 Try to figure out the literary reference.

Everything in this book has been included to celebrate and delight bibliophiles. If you see a page you don't quite understand, it's there to bring you a moment of bookish joy . . . if you can figure out what it means. While most of our four-digit extension codes lead to stories about books, some of them will reveal the voices behind literary projects that we love. Check back often, as we'll continuously update many extensions in this Phone Book as time goes by.

How to use this book to celebrate books

This book is full of invitations to get involved with *Call Me Ishmael.* If one of our prompts or another reader's story inspires you, call 774-325-0503 and leave us a message of your own.

CALLS *by* SUBJECT

Adventures

An anonymous voicemail message about

Arabian Sands by Wilfred Thesiger

Ext. 4660

Hi, this is Rinker Buck. I'm the author of *Flight of Passage* and *The Oregon Trail: A New American Journey*, and the best book in the English language is Wilfred Thesiger's *Arabian Sands*, followed closely by Wilfred Thesiger's *The Marsh Arabs*. Wilfred Thesiger was one of the last great British explorers of the Victorian era, although he did his best work in the 1940s and 1950s. In the late forties, after serving pretty valiantly in World War II as a British Special Operations Officer in Arabia, he stayed behind and took a camel ride with a bunch of bedouin nomads through the so-called Empty Quarter in Saudi Arabia. This was before Saudi Arabia developed into the modern kingdom that we know today; it was totally absent of any modern conveniences in the old bedouin lifestyle. Wilfred Thesiger spent five years roaming the Empty Quarter—the desert—with a group of bedouins and wrote one of the most memorable and beautiful tales of all time. *The Marsh Arabs* is about his time spent in the marshes just north of Basra along the Euphrates River, before Saddam Hussein destroyed the marshes to chase the Marsh Arabs out because they weren't loyal to him. Anyway, Thesiger is just a fabulous writer, completely unpretentious and clearly detailed in describing the wonder of travel in such remote places. I can't say enough about those two books and I can't say enough about Wilfred Thesiger. He died after roaming the world, and really accomplished in the twentieth century what many of us associate with the wandering Victorians of the nineteenth century. He died at the age of ninety-four, and those two books will just introduce you to the beauty and the wonder of spirited, rugged travel. When there are years when you don't get out to do anything—you don't go out to do any adventuring, it's terrible—you have to write a book that year. And so we all need that kind of Walter Mitty escape and I can only recommend to this audience—the Ishmael audience—I can recommend Wilfred Thesiger as quite possibly the best writer ever. That's hyperbole, but when you really love a writer, you're entitled to a little bit of hyperbole. ☎

An anonymous voicemail message about

Harry Potter series by J. K. Rowling

Ext. 2111

Hey, Ishmael. I'd like to plug the most influential young adult series of my generation, which you can probably guess is the Harry Potter series by J. K. Rowling. I grew up with a single mother who was hopelessly addicted to crack. It was a brutal time for me. She would frequently go on binges for days on end, leaving me alone—or worse, in the company of dangerous people. After, she would always buy me a jawbreaker candy or a yo-yo or some other cheap trinket to show me that she was sorry. The trinkets could never replace her love or a normal childhood, but after one binge on my eleventh birthday, she bought me a copy of *Harry Potter and the Sorcerer's Stone*. I spent the next seven years spellbound. I like to think the series was my patronus, what I used to keep the darkness from getting in. Like Harry, I knew what it was like to hide in the cupboard and to be abused by the people charged with caring for you. So, I allowed myself the belief those years that if Harry could be rescued, so could I. The series provided the bubble I needed to survive my childhood, and because of it I'm honestly far less emotionally scarred now than I would've been. My name is Nathan and I'm the boy who lived. Thanks for taking my call, Ishmael. ☎

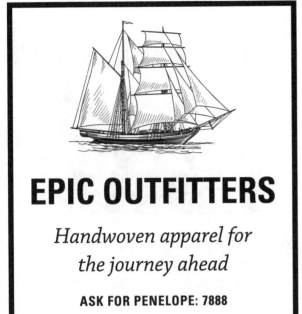

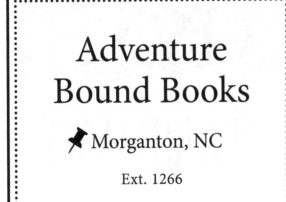

Adversity

Advice

Tralfamadorian Therapy

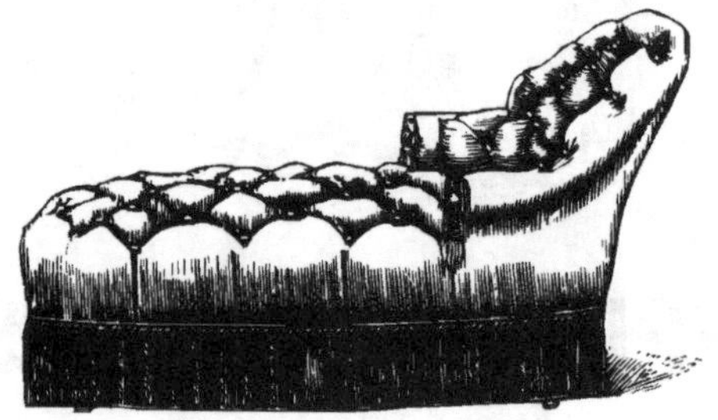

We'll change your worldview

Book anytime with Billy: 8007

Group counselor for hire.
Bring yourself and your friends.

Let's meet when life gets dire
at the place where the sidewalk ends.

Ext. 1950

BIBLIOTHERAPY

RECOMMENDED READINGS AND REMEDIES

Ext. 3446

 To hear any of these stories, dial 774-325-0503 and dial the four-digit extension.

Airplanes

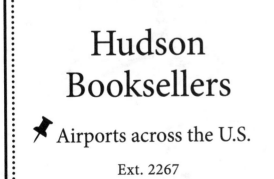

An anonymous voicemail message about

Cutting for Stone
by Abraham Verghese

Ext. 6578

Hey, Ishmael. I'm calling to tell you a story about a book that I read on a long flight, called *Cutting for Stone* by Abraham Verghese. A friend of mine had recently given it to me, and I was about three-fourths of the way through the book when I noticed the woman across the aisle starting to get restless. She stands up and she opens the overhead compartment and she moves her jacket and then she starts to zip a lot of zippers in her carry-on, and finally she pulls out this little pouch that she puts on her seat. And then she starts to put everything away, and then finally she sits back down, very still. So eventually I forgot about her and kept reading. And I read and I read, totally engrossed in this extraordinary story about twins and family and devotion and humanity, when all of a sudden I hit a stretch of narrative that just totally wrecked me. And I start sobbing—and I mean like complete shameless snot-flowing-down-my-face kind of sobbing. It was really embarrassing. But then this woman that I had noticed earlier opened the little pouch that she had retrieved from her bag and pulls out a tissue, and when she hands it to me she says, "I read that book a few weeks ago and I knew you were getting close." I was stunned and grateful. She knew I would need the tissue when she saw me open that book at the very beginning of the flight. I think about that now every time I read on the plane. Goodbye. ☎

ALABAMA BOOKSTORES

- ❑ 1977 Books: Montgomery
- ❑ Alabama Booksmith: Homewood
- ❑ Auburn Oil Co. Booksellers: Auburn
- ❑ Church Street Coffee and Books: Mountain Brook
- ❑ Ernest & Hadley Booksellers: Tuscaloosa
- ❑ Fae Crate: Wetumpka
- ❑ Little Professor Book Center: Homewood
- ❑ NewSouth Books: Montgomery
- ❑ Ol' Curiosities & Book Shoppe: Monroeville
- ❑ Page and Palette: Fairhope
- ❑ The Haunted Book Shop: Mobile
- ❑ The Snail on the Wall: Huntsville
- ❑ Woni's Bookshelf: Sumiton

Alabama

Just Mercy by Bryan Stevenson..............................5755
Looking for Alaska by John Green 5769
Looking for Alaska by John Green 9201
To Kill a Mockingbird by Harper Lee........................4933
To Kill a Mockingbird by Harper Lee........................6346

INTERVIEWS WITH ALABAMA BOOKSTORES

Ext. 3497

Listen to stories from some of our favorite bookshops in Alabama.

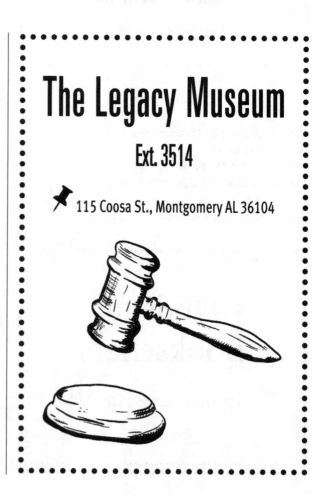

The Legacy Museum

Ext. 3514

115 Coosa St., Montgomery AL 36104

 To hear any of these stories, dial 774-325-0503 and dial the four-digit extension.

at the Fitzgerald House Museum

Ext. 6453

919 Felder Ave.
Montgomery, AL 36106

ALASKA BOOKSTORES

- ❑ Arctic Loon Co.: Kokhanok
- ❑ Fireside Books: Palmer
- ❑ Hearthside Books: Juneau
- ❑ Hearthside Books & Toys at Nugget Mall: Juneau
- ❑ Homer Bookstore: Homer
- ❑ Old Harbor Books: Sitka
- ❑ Parnassus Books: Ketchikan
- ❑ River City Books: Soldotna
- ❑ Skaguay News Depot & Books: Skagway
- ❑ The Islander Bookshop: Kodiak
- ❑ The Writer's Block Bookstore & Cafe: Anchorage
- ❑ Title Wave Books: Anchorage

Alaska

Into the Wild by Jon Krakauer.................................7744
The Call of the Wild by Jack London.........................4938
White Fang by Jack London 9769

49th State Brewing

Ext. 1753

717 W. 3rd Ave., Healy, AK 99501

INTERVIEWS WITH ALASKA BOOKSTORES

Ext. 4398

Listen to stories from some of our favorite bookshops in Alaska.

Ancestors

Angela's Ashes by Frank McCourt 7842
Sabrina and Corina by Kali Fajardo-Anstine 2268
Women Who Run with the Wolves by Clarissa Pinkola Estés 1640

Anger

Animal Farm by George Orwell...............................1029
Ariel by Sylvia Plath..4661
Carrie by Stephen King...5676
I Am Malala by Malala Yousafzai 8888
Invisible Man by Ralph Ellison 1235
The Darkest Child by Delores Phillips 4847
The Monkey Wrench Gang by Edward Abbey...........7559

Animals

Black Beauty by Anna Sewell.................................5669
Crime and Punishment by Fyodor Dostoyevsky.......7550
Dinnertime by Jan Pieńkowski 4592
Moby-Dick by Herman Melville................................3778
My Family and Other Animals by Gerald Durrell 7576
Northern Lights by Philip Pullman 3787
The Dogs of Babel by Carolyn Parkhurst 7689

RENT A RAGE ROOM

A safe space to smash stuff.
BYO monkey wrench.

Reserve today with
Hayduke: 7559

Lion's Mouth Bookstore

Green Bay, WI

Ext. 2768

Lyra's Animal Training

Is your furry friend a dæmon?
We'll help it settle down.

CALL FOR APPOINTMENTS: 3787

 To hear any of these stories, dial 774-325-0503 and dial the four-digit extension.

Ahab's Whale Tours

GUARANTEED SIGHTING ON THE FIRST (AND ONLY!) LEG OF YOUR TRIP.

Book today: 3778

The Parrot's Lament by Eugene Linden 7892
The Sibley Guide to Birds by David Allen Sibley......9908
The Tale of Despereaux by Kate DiCamillo...............6922
Watership Down by Richard Adams 7844
We Are All Completely Beside Ourselves by
Karen Joy Fowler 3940

Penguin Bookshop

Sewickley, PA

Ext. 2969

Sewell's Stables

Visit our equestrian center—it's a beauty!

Call: 5669

HAZEL'S HABITATS

Crates! Aquariums! Doghouses!

Get your pet a safe new home for just 20% down!

Ext. 7844

Anxiety

Infinite Jest by David Foster Wallace 7560
Moby-Dick by Herman Melville................................2112
Narcissus and Goldmund by Hermann Hesse..........3785
What Do You Do with an Idea? by Kobi Yamada 2942

Arizona

Stargirl by Jerry Spinelli...1009
The Monkey Wrench Gang by Edward Abbey...........7559

Rúla Búla

Ext. 4170

401 S. Mill Ave.
Tempe, AZ 85281

Cherokee Elementary School

Ext. 2002

Paradise Valley, AZ

 To hear any of these stories, dial 774-325-0503 and dial the four-digit extension.

ARIZONA BOOKSTORES

- ❑ Anticus: Scottsdale
- ❑ Antigone Books: Tucson
- ❑ Bisbee Books & Music: Bisbee
- ❑ Bonny Books: Mesa
- ❑ Bookmans Entertainment Exchange: Flagstaff, Mesa, Phoenix, Tucson
- ❑ Bright Side Bookshop: Flagstaff
- ❑ Changing Hands Bookstore: Phoenix, Tempe
- ❑ Clues Unlimited: Tucson
- ❑ Copper News Bookstore: Ajo
- ❑ Enchanted Chapters: Phoenix
- ❑ Get Lit. Books: Sierra Vista
- ❑ Guidon Books: Scottsdale
- ❑ Half Price Books: Camelback, Paradise Valley, Mesa
- ❑ Mary Ann's Mostly Books: Apache Junction
- ❑ Mostly Books: Tucson
- ❑ My Cat Jeoffry Bookstore and Cat Lounge: Chandler
- ❑ Palabras Bilingual Bookstore: Phoenix
- ❑ Peregrine Book Company: Prescott
- ❑ R Bookmark: Youngtown
- ❑ Red-Tail Books: Casa Grande
- ❑ Revolutionary Grounds Books & Coffee: Tucson
- ❑ Sun Devil Marketplace: Tempe
- ❑ The Book Haven: Prescott Valley
- ❑ The Book Shop: Green Valley
- ❑ The Literate Lizard: Sedona
- ❑ The Poisoned Pen Bookstore: Scottsdale

INTERVIEWS WITH ARIZONA BOOKSTORES

Ext. 1199

Listen to stories from some of our favorite bookshops in Arizona.

Arkansas

Maya Angelou City Park

Stamps, AR

Ext. 1282

ARKANSAS BOOKSTORES

- ❑ Bookish: An Indie Shop for Folks Who Read: Fort Smith
- ❑ Chapters on Main: Van Buren
- ❑ Dog Ear Books: Russellville
- ❑ It's A Mystery BookStore: Berryville
- ❑ Jefferson Street Books: El Dorado
- ❑ Nightbird Books: Fayetteville
- ❑ Pyramid Art, Books & Custom Framing: Little Rock
- ❑ River Bend Books: Little Rock
- ❑ That Bookstore in Blytheville: Blytheville
- ❑ Two Friends Bookstore: Bentonville
- ❑ WordsWorth Books: Little Rock

INTERVIEWS WITH ARKANSAS BOOKSTORES

Ext. 1299

Listen to stories from some of our favorite bookshops in Arkansas.

Art

Atlas of Human Anatomy for the Artist by Stephen Rogers Peck....4596
Boom by Michael Shnayerson....5671
Just Kids by Patti Smith....6754
Maus by Art Spiegelman....4454
Merriam-Webster's Collegiate Dictionary....4445
Sex Criminals by Matt Fraction and Chip Zdarsky....7838
Steal Like an Artist by Austin Kleon....1825
The Art Lesson by Tomie dePaola....2834
The Art Spirit by Robert Henri....2356
The Wonderful Wizard of Oz by L. Frank Baum....5926

 To hear any of these stories, dial 774-325-0503 and dial the four-digit extension.

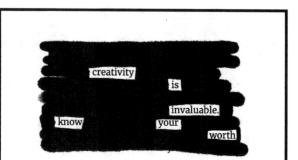

JUST KILNS

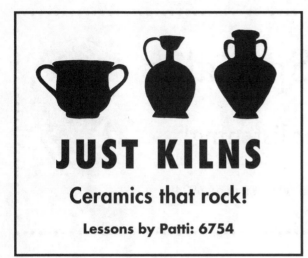

Ceramics that rock!

Lessons by Patti: 6754

Audiobooks

Live Models

Master the art of figure drawing

Ext. 4596

EXTREME AUDIO SOLUTIONS

Out of this world service. Home of the original ear spuds.

Contact Mark: 1051

An anonymous voicemail message about

The Night Circus by Erin Morgenstern

Ext. 4606

Hi, Ishmael. So here is my story: My mom and I went on a very long cross-country road trip because she offered to let me keep the family car at college and I needed someone to drive the car down with. We decided to check out an audiobook from the library for our trip, and the book we chose was *The Night Circus* by Erin Morgenstern, because the narrator was the same guy who narrated the Harry Potter audiobooks, which we love. Well, my mom and I both fell in love with this book. It is magical, captivating, and perfect in so many ways that I don't want to spoil. But, when we got to the end of the trip, we still had a lot of the audiobook left and my mom had to fly home and return it to the library. Well, I had to know what happened next, so I checked out the book on my library e-reader app on my tablet, quickly devoured the rest of it, and it ended up being my favorite book that I read in 2014—well, I guess I half read, half listened to it. But anyway, when I returned from college for the holidays I found in my bedroom a beautiful copy of *The Night Circus* sitting on my bed. My mom told me she knew how much I loved physical books. She had found this gorgeous copy, and even though it was kind of expensive, she thought it was worth it. After further questioning I found that she had returned the audiobook to the library and couldn't wait to finish the book either and had bought this copy that we could now treasure forever. And that is my story. Thanks, Ishmael. 

Authors

"What really knocks me out is a book that, when you're all done reading it, you wish the author that wrote it was a terrific friend of yours and you could call him up on the phone whenever you felt like it."

—*The Catcher in the Rye* by J. D. Salinger

Ext. 1391

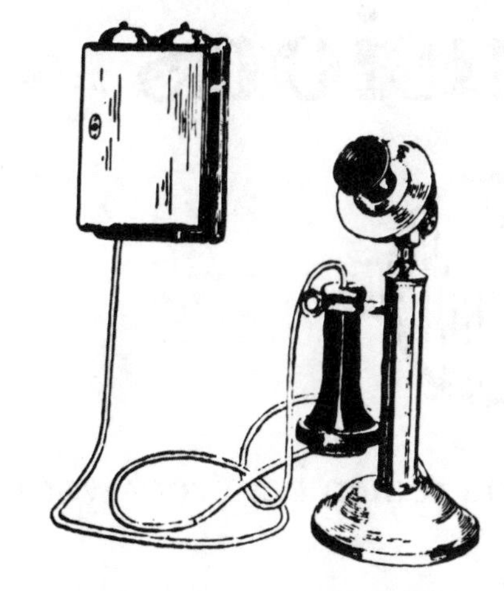

Call about an author you wish everyone knew.

Ext. 2192

Magical Bookshelf Emporium

Hands-free delivery and assembly.

Ask for Matilda: 9837

Avid Readers

A Little Princess by Frances Hodgson Burnett..........6878
Bridge to Terabithia by Katherine Paterson.............4959
Icy Sparks by Gwyn Hyman Rubio...........................7740
Matilda by Roald Dahl..7837
The Eye of the World series by Robert Jordan..........4351
The Giver by Lois Lowry...5854
The Secret History by Donna Tartt...........................9768

AVID
READER
PRESS

Avid Readers

Ext. 2793

Optical Allusions

Color-enhancing bifocals that will help you remember every word.

Ask for Jonas: 5854

Bars and Pubs

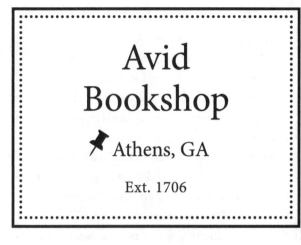

Beach Reads

Beauty

An anonymous voicemail message about

Frankenstein by Mary Shelley

Ext. 9999

When asked to pick a book that I love or has impacted me, I couldn't help but think about Mary Shelley's *Frankenstein.* I actually read this book twice, once as an eleventh grader in my English class and then again as a freshman in college in my Composition II course. This book first stuck out for me because of my ability to connect with Dr. Victor Frankenstein and his depression. As an eleventh grader I had been suffering with depression for several years. I attempted suicide during my fall semester and reread this book during my spring semester. I could identify with the feelings Victor had over losing William and Justine, since I had just lost my mother a few years earlier. Feeling guilty over my mother's death, I looked for comfort in food and had an unhealthy obsession with it. I also felt a strong connection with Dr. Frankenstein's monster. Around this time in high school, I weighed around 320 pounds and felt like a monster myself. As I walked through the halls of school, I felt my fellow students staring at me. I would even hear them call me names when they weren't. When I started therapy, my psychiatrist started me on a medication. [Soon I realized] that my classmates and complete strangers, who I thought were staring at me and calling me names actually weren't at all. It was a manifestation in my mind. I not only saw myself as a monster from the outside, but I thought everyone else also saw me as a monster. I have since been able to lose over two hundred pounds in the last few years. I have recently undergone surgery to remove excess skin and have scars from that surgery all over my body. Oddly enough, I now have the scars to look like Dr. Frankenstein's monster. ☎

Gray's Portraits

Unlock the beauty within

Call: 9899

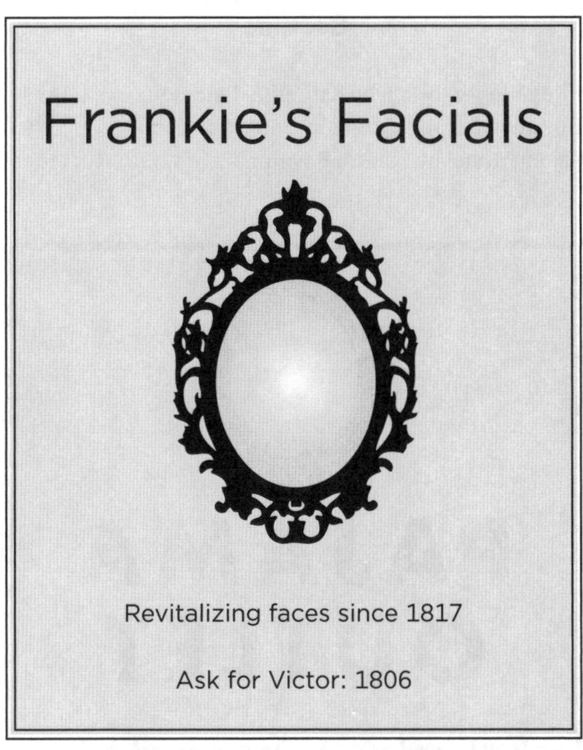

Becoming a Reader

A Little Princess by Frances Hodgson Burnett.........6878
Eragon by Christopher Paolini...............................4602
Escaping the Giant Wave by Peg Kehret.................7696
Harry Potter and the Sorcerer's Stone by J. K. Rowling...5347
Holes by Louis Sachar...6801
Inkheart trilogy by Cornelia Funke.........................8680
Mr. Popper's Penguins by Richard and Florence Atwater...3779
My Louisiana Sky by Kimberly Willis Holt................1014
Northern Lights by Philip Pullman..........................3787
The Book Thief by Markus Zusak............................1060
The Hobbit by J. R. R. Tolkien................................9003
The Library Book by Susan Orlean..........................4444
Well-Read Black Girl by Glory Edim........................4019
Zlateh the Goat and Other Stories by Isaac Bashevis Singer..4958

Rubeus's Reading Hut

Creating giant readers.
Pets welcome.

Book here: 5347

To hear any of these stories, dial 774-325-0503 and dial the four-digit extension.

An anonymous voicemail message about

The Book Thief
by Markus Zusak

Ext. 1060

There I was: twelve years old, incredibly intimidated by the size of *The Book Thief*, and struggling a bit over pronunciation. But I carried on. I was twelve when I first got it, and I was twelve when I first learned how much a book could hurt you. How fiction is fatal and how much you can cry over it. Twelve when I realized how beautiful words can be and how much a story matters to someone and everyone. Its take on Death is poised and eye-opening. It's my favorite stand-alone, and the only historical fiction I've read to this day. I was twelve when I got my first existential crisis and I was twelve when I fell in love with words. ☎

Bedtime

Better Than the Movie

 To hear any of these stories, dial 774-325-0503 and dial the four-digit extension.

Ebenezer's VHS Rental

Provide read-receipts upon entry.
All late fees diligently accounted for,
every one.

Open on Christmas.

Ext. 1641

To hear any of these stories, dial 774-325-0503 and dial the four-digit extension.

Bibliophiles

Inkheart trilogy by Cornelia Funke 8680
Kushiel's Dart by Jacqueline Carey 5756
Mr. Popper's Penguins by Richard and Florence Atwater 3779
Sabriel by Garth Nix 1809
The Littles to the Rescue by John Peterson 6879

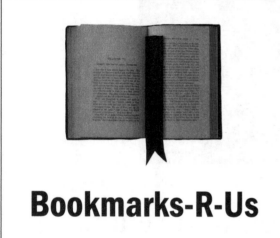

Big Questions, Asking the

32 Candles by Ernessa T. Carter 7553
A Short History of Nearly Everything by Bill Bryson 7722
All Quiet on the Western Front by Erich Maria Remarque 3653

An anonymous voicemail message about

Jurassic Park by Michael Crichton

Ext. 2001

The book that changed my view of the natural world was Michael Crichton's *Jurassic Park.* I did read the book before I saw the movie, so I went into that with a better understanding than most people, probably. I was reading it in eighth grade and it was just about the time when I was starting to think philosophically. I was in all of these classes that were very thought-provoking, and just about this time when I was reading *Jurassic Park* I started to see some of the world's mathematical and biological implications. I had mostly thought of life on earth as this big coincidence, but as I read through *Jurassic Park,* I learned life is resilient enough that it can exist wherever the conditions are correct. And it will almost immediately pop into existence wherever those conditions are met. I started to see the world through this lens of event patterns of inevitability. It really opened up the world and made everything seem more beautiful to me. So *Jurassic Park* truly did change my life. ☎

Book Clubs

Book clubs we wish we were a part of: 9876

Have a great book club? We want to feature you!

Say hi:

ishmael@callmeishmael.com

Book Covers

An anonymous voicemail message about

Prep
by Curtis Sittenfeld

Ext. 1050

Hi, Ishmael. I wanted to talk about a book called *Prep*. It's by Curtis Sittenfeld. I read it my sophomore year of high school. I was in a class that, it was a really great class—you just basically read whatever you wanted and then wrote about it. And I just wanted sort of like a book that could turn my mind off for a little bit. So I picked this up because it looked like one of those books. I judged it by its cover, because that's what you do. It ended up sort of saving my life. On every page I would find things that this narrator thought that I had thought earlier that day. You know, like so many high schoolers, I thought I was completely alone and I had the strangest thoughts and I was just this crazy person. This book was just a wake-up call for me. It was like, *Wow. I'm not insane. I'm not that . . . You know . . . Special.* But it was a fantastic experience. When I had to write about the book for the class, I had to say whether or not I recommended it. And I said, "I love this book, but I would never recommend it to anybody because I feel like once they read it they would know too much about me." I wanted to thank the author for giving me that experience. ☎

Call and tell us about a time you judged a book by its cover.

Ext. 5877

Captain Underpants series by Dav Pilkey................6026
Harry Potter and the Sorcerer's Stone by
J. K. Rowling...5347
The Mozart Season by Virginia Euwer Wolff 7884
The Wonderful Wizard of Oz by L. Frank Baum.........5926
To Kill a Mockingbird by Harper Lee 5813

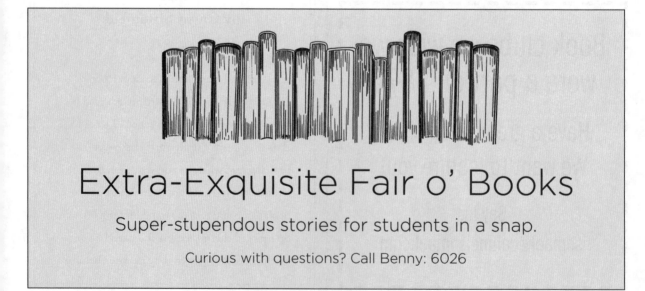

Extra-Exquisite Fair o' Books

Super-stupendous stories for students in a snap.

Curious with questions? Call Benny: 6026

Booksellers

Bloodroot by Amy Greene 4961
Charlotte by David Foenkinos 6679
In the Kingdom of Ice by Hampton Sides 7742
The Book of Disquiet by Fernando Pessoa..............9956
The Shining Girls by Lauren Beukes.......................9906
The Storied Life of A. J. Fikry by Gabrielle Zevin 7914
Wuthering Heights by Emily Brontë 9537

Bookstores

A Man Called Ove by Fredrik Backman 2645
A Supposedly Fun Thing I'll Never Do Again by David Foster Wallace 1963
Charlotte by David Foenkinos 6679
Guts by Chuck Palahniuk.......................................1533
Homegoing by Yaa Gyasi...7201
I'm with the Band by Pamela Des Barres................7739
In a Dark, Dark Wood by Ruth Ware.........................1038
In the Kingdom of Ice by Hampton Sides 7742
On the Road by Jack Kerouac 2796
Quest for the Lost City by Dana and Ginger Lamb ...2800
Song of Solomon by Toni Morrison 9939
The Art of Fielding by Chad Harbach 1006
The Art of Racing in the Rain by Garth Stein............7204
The Eye of the World series by Robert Jordan 4351
The Fan Man by William Kotzwinkle 7556
The Middle Stories by Sheila Heti 9001
The Spirit of Fairhope by Dean and Megrez R. Mosher...8910

Flourish and Blotts

Ext. 2438

All Our Books Are Magic

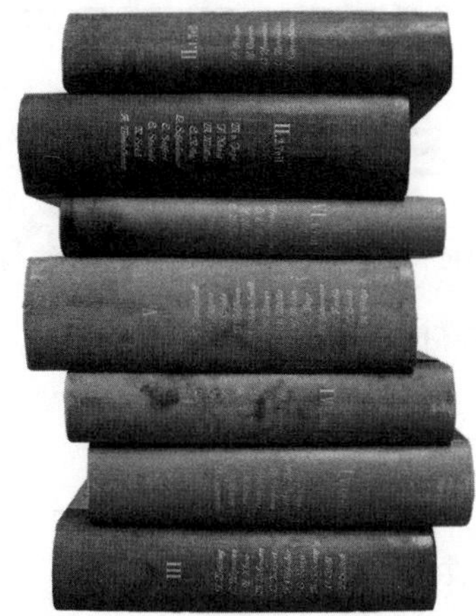

Island Books

Alice Island's only bookshop!

We're hiring—Come inquire with A.J.

Ext. 4339

Monsieur Labisse

– BOOKSHOP –

Ext. 5487

Time for books, s'il vous plaît.

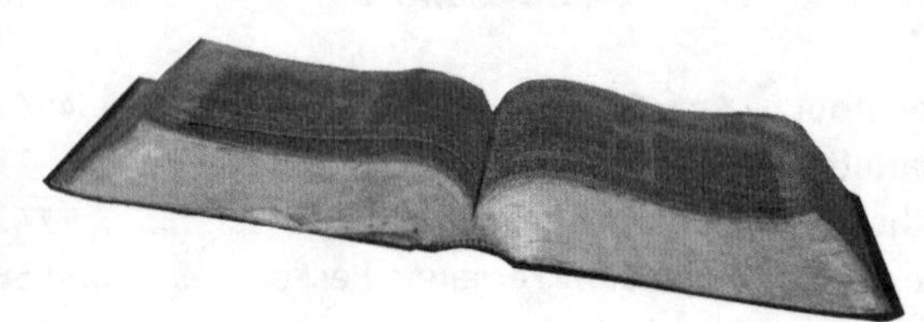

BOOKSTORE IN SAN FRANCISCO

OPEN 24 HOURS

Ext. 9372

Special requests?
Come by and ask for Ajax.

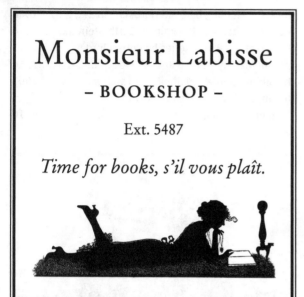

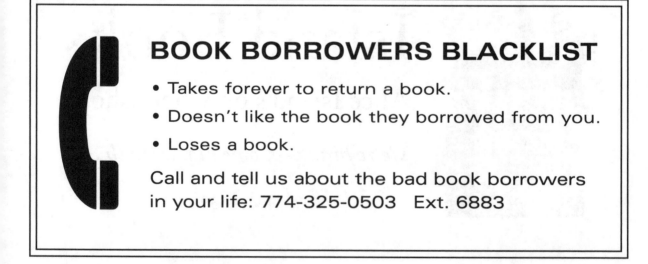

Borrowed Books

Broken by Daniel Clay....5674
I'll Give You the Sun by Jandy Nelson....4610
Strawberry Fields by Marina Lewycka....2830
The Hitchhiker's Guide to the Galaxy by Douglas Adams....4242

BOOK BORROWERS BLACKLIST

- Takes forever to return a book.
- Doesn't like the book they borrowed from you.
- Loses a book.

Call and tell us about the bad book borrowers in your life: 774-325-0503 Ext. 6883

Bullies

A Series of Unfortunate Events by Lemony Snicket 8635
American Born Chinese by Gene Luen Yang 5490
Atlas of World History edited by Patrick K. O'Brien ... 1030
Bully.com by Joe Lawlor 2365
I Like Me! by Nancy Carlson 5001
Junie B. Jones Is a Party Animal by Barbara Park 6753
The Hitchhiker's Guide to the Galaxy by Douglas Adams 6870
The Hobbit by J. R. R. Tolkien 9003
The Mother-Daughter Book Club by Heather Vogel Frederick 7883
Thirteen Reasons Why by Jay Asher 1052
Wonder by R. J. Palacio 2956

Oak 'n Shield Securities

13 bodyguards at your beck and call.

Ask for Thorin: 9003

California, Northern

American Born Chinese by Gene Luen Yang............1025
American Born Chinese by Gene Luen Yang............5490
Cannery Row by John Steinbeck.............................5497
Do Androids Dream of Electric Sheep?
by Philip K. Dick..7687
Do Androids Dream of Electric Sheep?
by Philip K. Dick..7688
Little Brother by Cory Doctorow.............................5762
Of Mice and Men by John Steinbeck........................3788
The Joy Luck Club by Amy Tan 7749
The Man Who Loved Books Too Much by
Allison Hoover Bartlett.......................................6880

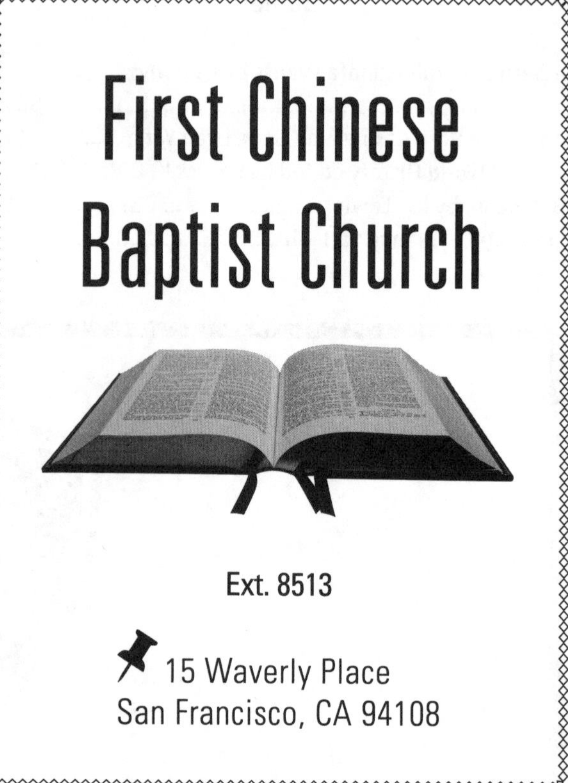

First Chinese
Baptist Church
Ext. 8513
15 Waverly Place
San Francisco, CA 94108

INTERVIEWS WITH NORTHERN CALIFORNIA BOOKSTORES

Ext. 6434

Listen to stories from some of our favorite bookshops in Northern California.

Henry Miller
Memorial Library
Ext. 5626
48603 CA-1, Big Sur, CA 93920

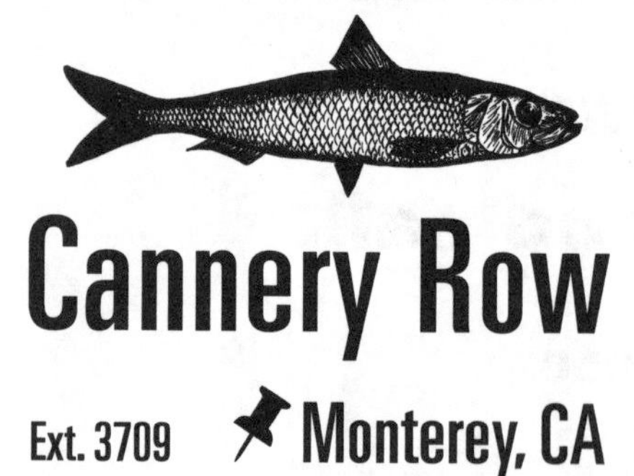

NORTHERN CALIFORNIA BOOKSTORES

- ❑ A Great Good Place for Books: Oakland
- ❑ A Seat at the Table Books: Elk Grove
- ❑ Afikomen Judaica: Berkeley
- ❑ Alexander Book Company: San Francisco
- ❑ Alibi Bookshop: Vallejo
- ❑ All Things Book: Windsor
- ❑ Alley Cat Bookstore & Gallery: San Francisco
- ❑ Amoeba Music: Berkeley, San Francisco
- ❑ Ashay by the Bay: Vallejo
- ❑ Avid Reader Active: Davis
- ❑ B & B Booksellers: Chester
- ❑ Bandung Books: Oakland
- ❑ Barn Owl Books: Quincy
- ❑ Bay Tree Bookstore: Santa Cruz
- ❑ Beers Books: Sacramento
- ❑ Bel and Bunna's Books: Lafayette
- ❑ Bell's Books: Palo Alto
- ❑ Bethel Store: Redding
- ❑ Bird & Beckett Books and Records: San Francisco
- ❑ Black Bird Bookstore: San Francisco
- ❑ Book Passage: Corte Madera, San Francisco
- ❑ Books Inc.: Alameda, Berkeley, Campbell, Laurel Village, Mountain View, Opera Plaza, Palo Alto, The Marina, San Francisco
- ❑ Books on B: Hayward
- ❑ Books on Main: Murphys
- ❑ Bookshop Benicia: Benicia
- ❑ Bookshop Santa Cruz: Santa Cruz
- ❑ Bookshop West Portal: San Francisco
- ❑ BookSmart: Morgan Hill
- ❑ Booky Joint: Mammoth Lakes
- ❑ Branches Books & Gifts: Oakhurst
- ❑ Browser Books: San Francisco
- ❑ Builders Booksource: Berkeley
- ❑ Capital Books: Sacramento
- ❑ Charlie's Corner: San Francisco
- ❑ Christopher's Books: San Francisco
- ❑ City Lights Bookstore: San Francisco
- ❑ Coastside Books, Inc.: Half Moon Bay
- ❑ Copperfield's Books: Calistoga, Healdsburg, Larkspur, Montgomery Village, Napa, Novato, Petaluma, San Rafael, Sebastopol
- ❑ Dog Eared Books: San Francisco
- ❑ Downtown Book & Sound: Salinas
- ❑ East Bay Booksellers: Oakland
- ❑ Eastwind Books of Berkeley: Berkeley
- ❑ Ecology Center: Berkeley
- ❑ Eureka Books: Eureka
- ❑ Face in a Book: El Dorado Hills
- ❑ Fields Book Store: El Cerrito
- ❑ Flashlight Books: Walnut Creek
- ❑ Folio Books: San Francisco
- ❑ Four-Eyed Frog Books: Gualala
- ❑ Gallery Bookshop & Bookwinkle's Children's Books: Mendocino
- ❑ Globus Books: San Francisco
- ❑ Green Apple Books: San Francisco

NORTHERN CALIFORNIA BOOKSTORES (CONT.)

- ❑ Half Price Books: Berkeley, Citrus Heights, Concord, Dublin, Fremont
- ❑ Hicklebee's: San Jose
- ❑ Hideaway Books: Sacramento
- ❑ Ink Spell Books: Half Moon Bay
- ❑ Jenny's Paper & Ink Books: Grass Valley
- ❑ Kepler's Books: Menlo Park
- ❑ Kinokuniya: San Francisco
- ❑ Laurel Book Store: Oakland
- ❑ Libreria Pino: San Francisco
- ❑ Linden Tree Children's Books: Los Altos
- ❑ Main Street Bookmine: St. Helena
- ❑ Margie's Book Nook: Susanville
- ❑ Mendocino Book Company: Ukiah
- ❑ Miranda Culp: San Francisco
- ❑ Moe's Books: Berkeley
- ❑ Mountain Bookshop: Sonora
- ❑ Mr. Mopps' Children's Books: Berkeley
- ❑ Mrs. Dalloway's Literary & Garden Arts: Berkeley
- ❑ Napa Bookmine: Napa
- ❑ Northtown Books: Arcata
- ❑ Orinda Books: Orinda
- ❑ Pages Books on the Green: Windsor
- ❑ Pegasus Books Oakland: Oakland
- ❑ Pegasus Books on Solano: Berkeley
- ❑ Petunia's Place: Fresno
- ❑ Pilgrim's Way Books: Carmel-by-the-Sea
- ❑ Placerville News Company: Placerville
- ❑ Point Reyes Books: Point Reyes Station
- ❑ Rakestraw Books: Danville
- ❑ Reach & Teach: San Mateo
- ❑ Readers' Books: Sonoma
- ❑ Real Books: Fairfield
- ❑ Recycle Bookstore: Campbell
- ❑ Revolution Books: Berkeley
- ❑ River House Books: Carmel-by-the-Sea
- ❑ Russian Hill Bookstore: San Francisco
- ❑ Sausalito Books by the Bay: Sausalito
- ❑ Shen's Books: Walnut Creek
- ❑ Sleepy Cat Books: Berkeley
- ❑ Spellbinder Books: Bishop
- ❑ Stinson Beach Books: Stinson Beach
- ❑ Sunlight of the Spirit: Sacramento
- ❑ The Avid Reader: Davis
- ❑ The Avid Reader on Broadway: Sacramento
- ❑ The Bindery: San Francisco
- ❑ The Book Juggler: Willits
- ❑ The Book Seller: Grass Valley
- ❑ The Book Tree in Montclair Village: Oakland
- ❑ The Booksmith: San Francisco
- ❑ The Collective: Oakland
- ❑ The Green Arcade: San Francisco
- ❑ The Reading Bug: San Carlos
- ❑ The Works: Pacific Grove
- ❑ Tin Can Mailman: Arcata
- ❑ Towne Center Books: Livermore, Pleasanton
- ❑ Twice Told Books: Guerneville
- ❑ Underground Books: Sacramento
- ❑ University Press Books: Berkeley
- ❑ Village Books: Ukiah
- ❑ Walden Pond Books: Oakland
- ❑ Winston Smith Books: Auburn
- ❑ Word After Word Books: Truckee
- ❑ Wow Cool Alternative Comics: Cupertino

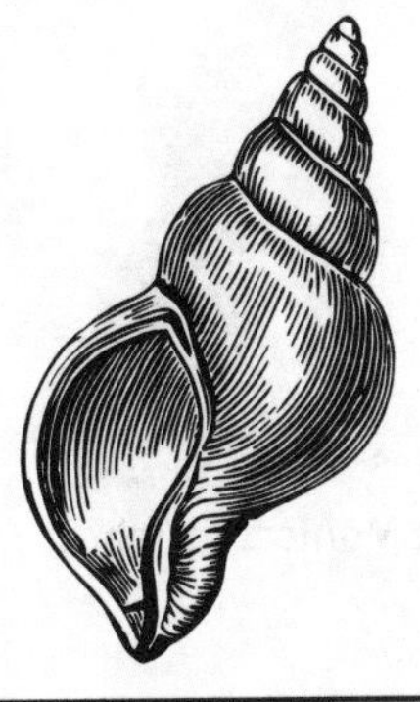

Coronado Public Library

Ext. 7227

640 Orange Ave., Coronado, CA 92118

California, Southern

Joan Didion's former Hollywood house

Ext. 6973

7406 Franklin Ave.
Los Angeles, CA 90046

INTERVIEWS WITH SOUTHERN CALIFORNIA BOOKSTORES

Ext. 2335

Listen to stories from some of our favorite bookshops in Southern California.

Central Library

Ext. 8934

630 W. 5th St.
Los Angeles, CA 90071

To hear any of these stories, dial 774-325-0503 and dial the four-digit extension.

SOUTHERN CALIFORNIA BOOKSTORES

- ❑ A Classic Tale: Ramona
- ❑ Abednego Book Shoppe: Ventura
- ❑ Acorn Naturalists: Tustin
- ❑ Adventure Ink: Pine Mountain Club
- ❑ Arcana: Books on the Arts: Culver City
- ❑ Artifact Books: Encinitas
- ❑ Authors Bookstore: Ontario
- ❑ Bank of Books: Ventura
- ❑ Bart's Books: Ojai
- ❑ Bay Books of Coronado at SAN: San Diego
- ❑ Bluestocking Books: San Diego
- ❑ Book Carnival: Orange
- ❑ Book Soup: West Hollywood
- ❑ BookMonster: Santa Monica
- ❑ BookPal: Irvine
- ❑ Books and Cookies: Santa Monica
- ❑ Bright Ideas Books: San Bernardino
- ❑ Burbank Military Books: Burbank
- ❑ Café Con Libros: Pomona
- ❑ Captain Fitch's Mercantile: San Diego
- ❑ Cellar Door Bookstore: Riverside
- ❑ Chaucer's Books: Santa Barbara
- ❑ Chevalier's Books: Los Angeles
- ❑ Children's Book World: Los Angeles
- ❑ Collector's Shangri-La: Los Angeles
- ❑ Comickaze Comics: Books and More!: San Diego
- ❑ Creating Conversations: Redondo Beach
- ❑ DIESEL, A Bookstore: Santa Monica, San Diego
- ❑ Eclectuals: Lakewood
- ❑ Eso Won Books: Los Angeles
- ❑ Flintridge Bookstore: La Cañada Flintridge
- ❑ Gatsby Books: Long Beach
- ❑ Hennessey & Ingalls: Los Angeles
- ❑ Kinokuniya: Los Angeles, Santa Monica, Torrence
- ❑ LA Libreria: Los Angeles
- ❑ La Playa Books: San Diego
- ❑ Laguna Beach Books: Laguna Beach
- ❑ Larry Edmunds Bookshop: Los Angeles
- ❑ Library Shop: San Diego
- ❑ Libreria: Los Angeles
- ❑ Lido Village Books: Newport Beach
- ❑ Little Fun Club: Glendale
- ❑ LowLead Books: Pasadena
- ❑ Malik Books: Los Angeles
- ❑ Mysterious Galaxy Bookstore: San Diego
- ❑ Mystery Ink: Huntington Beach
- ❑ Mystery Pier Books, Inc.: West Hollywood
- ❑ Mystic Journey Bookstore: Venice
- ❑ Newsboy Books: Ontario
- ❑ Once Upon a Storybook: Tustin
- ❑ Once Upon a Time: Montrose
- ❑ Pages: A Bookstore: Manhattan Beach
- ❑ Paradise Found: Santa Barbara
- ❑ Print and Page Booksellers: Crestline
- ❑ Rabbit Readers Children's Book Club: La Jolla
- ❑ Red Rock Books: Ridgecrest
- ❑ Robespierre Books: Solvang
- ❑ Run for Cover Bookstore: San Diego
- ❑ Russo's Books: Bakersfield
- ❑ San Marino Toy & Book Shoppe: San Marino
- ❑ Sandcastle Tales: Del Mar
- ❑ Sandpiper Books: Torrance
- ❑ Schwabe Books: Simi Valley
- ❑ Skylight Books: Los Angeles

SOUTHERN CALIFORNIA BOOKSTORES

- ❑ Small World Books: Venice
- ❑ Stories Books & Cafe: Los Angeles
- ❑ Tecolote Book Shop: Santa Barbara
- ❑ The Book Catapult: San Diego
- ❑ The Book Den: Santa Barbara
- ❑ The Book Jewel: Los Angeles
- ❑ The Book Loft: Solvang
- ❑ The Bookstore: Lompoc
- ❑ The Bookworm: Camarillo
- ❑ The Frugal Frigate: Redlands
- ❑ The Gamble House Bookstore: Pasadena
- ❑ The Getty Center Store: Los Angeles
- ❑ The Harvest Bookstore: Riverside
- ❑ The Iliad Bookshop: North Hollywood
- ❑ The Last Bookstore: Los Angeles
- ❑ The Lev: Venice
- ❑ The Ripped Bodice: Culver City
- ❑ Theodore Front Musical Literature: Santa Clarita
- ❑ Tía Chucha's Centro Cultural & Bookstore: Sylmar
- ❑ Vroman's Bookstore: Pasadena
- ❑ Vroman's Hastings Ranch: Pasadena
- ❑ Vroman's Newsstand: Pasadena
- ❑ Wandering Bookstore: Redondo Beach
- ❑ Warwick's: La Jolla

Career

13 Little Blue Envelopes by Maureen Johnson 3355
American Psycho by Bret Easton Ellis 4657
Atlas of Human Anatomy for the Artist by Stephen Rogers Peck 4596
Divergent by Veronica Roth....................................7579
Feed by Mira Grant 9324
Great Comedians Talk About Comedy by Larry Wilde 1440
Harriet the Spy by Louise Fitzhugh 8725
I Am Malala by Malala Yousafzai 5987
I'm with the Band by Pamela Des Barres................7739
In the Time of the Butterflies by Julia Alvarez..........8000
Little Brother by Cory Doctorow 5762
Mildred Pierce by James M. Cain............................4774
My Family and Other Animals by Gerald Durrell......7576
Sweetbitter by Stephanie Danler............................1827
The Art Lesson by Tomie dePaola..........................2834
The Glass Bead Game by Hermann Hesse 7818
The Parrot's Lament by Eugene Linden 7892
The Scarlet Letter by Nathaniel Hawthorne............9905
Tomorrow by Bradley Trevor Greive........................4934
Yes Please by Amy Poehler 3957

Childhood

A Little Princess by Frances Hodgson Burnett 6878
A Series of Unfortunate Events by Lemony Snicket ...7206
A Wrinkle in Time by Madeleine L'Engle 2359
Mrs. Piggle-Wiggle by Betty MacDonald 3781
The Friend by Sigrid Nunez 6857
The Hitchhiker's Guide to the Galaxy by Douglas Adams...4242
The House at Pooh Corner by A. A. Milne 4612
The Wind in the Willows by Kenneth Grahame 2582
To Kill a Mockingbird by Harper Lee 1964
Where the Sidewalk Ends by Shel Silverstein 1950

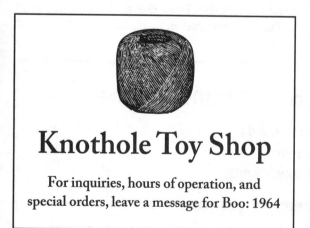

An anonymous voicemail message about

The Wind in the Willows by Kenneth Grahame

Ext. 2582

Hi, Ishmael. I'm calling to tell you about *The Wind in the Willows* by Kenneth Grahame. I read it when I was sixteen, and I found myself swept into the beauty of the English countryside and that little world by the river. I read it again and again. I just wanted to live in it. The thing is that, much later I really did live the book—but not in the way I expected. Like Portly the young otter, my two-year-old son vanished. We'd gone down to the mail room in our apartment building. I bent down to open the mailbox for a minute and when I turned around, he was gone. I rushed into the hall and into the street and I couldn't find him. He had completely disappeared. Five frantic minutes later—which really did feel like an eternity—he was found hiding behind a trash bin. We were grateful and we were lucky. He didn't even know he was missing. But he could have been snatched and he could have been lost to us. Yet somehow he was protected and returned. So the chapter I'm thinking about in *The Wind in the Willows* is "The Piper at the Gates of Dawn." The real shock of the chapter is that the life of the child away from the parent is actually better, more magical. So, as my children have grown and they've left for schools and camps and travels, I've always thought about the Piper keeping watch over them. The idea of the Piper at the Gates of Dawn watching out for my children out there is all these years later what's let me let them go and do what they have to do. Thank you very much. ☎

Collections

Babe & Me by Dan Gutman 3353
Boom by Michael Shnayerson 5671
Something Borrowed by Emily Giffin.......................1820
Texfake by W. Thomas Taylor.................................1005
The Giver by Lois Lowry 6860
The Great Gatsby by F. Scott Fitzgerald 6867
The Man Who Loved Books Too Much by
Allison Hoover Bartlett..6880

Olaf's Arcade

Maybe you'll win (you probably won't)

Call: 7206

Crook & Cranny

Rare books for sale.
Everything's a steal of a deal!

Call John Gilkey: 6880

SHADOW'S COIN SHOP

Count on us to complete your collection.

Closed on Wednesdays.

Ask for Sweeney: 2233

College

Ariel by Sylvia Plath....................4661
Franny and Zooey by J. D. Salinger....................9713
History of Plymouth Plantation by William Bradford....................1965
Let's Pretend This Never Happened by Jenny Lawson....................5760
Of Human Bondage by W. Somerset Maugham....................1668
Oh, the Places You'll Go! by Dr. Seuss....................9836
The Bell Jar by Sylvia Plath....................7577
The Opposite of Loneliness by Marina Keegan....................7548
The Sun Also Rises by Ernest Hemingway....................8913

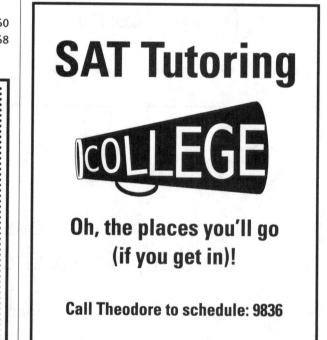

Midtown Scholar Bookstore

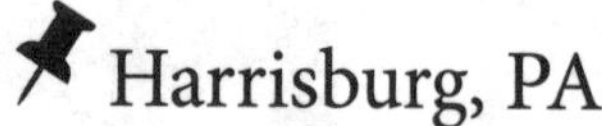

Ext. 3797

SAT Tutoring

Oh, the places you'll go (if you get in)!

Call Theodore to schedule: 9836

An anonymous voicemail message about

Of Human Bondage by W. Somerset Maugham

Ext. 1668

I read *Of Human Bondage* by W. Somerset Maugham in the summer of my freshman year of college. My freshman year of college was pretty rough on me; I came from a very rural area and went to school with a lot of people from a metropolitan area. They seemed so much more worldly than I was. I seemed very naive in comparison and it seemed their ideas were better formed than mine and their opinions more confident. It gave me great solace to find someone in a book who seemed to be facing some of the same issues that I was relative to relationships and the meaning of life in general. By no means do I imply that my life paralleled Philip Carey's! I did have a happy childhood—which Philip Carey did not—and I did not come to the same conclusions he did in addressing some of these life issues, but I think it's a very important thing to have an author who is better at articulating and interpreting issues that can in the long run provide great comfort and support and direction for someone who is not as worldly and maybe hasn't seen as many things in his life. *Of Human Bondage* did provide so much comfort and direction and solace for me. ☎

Colorado

INTERVIEWS WITH COLORADO BOOKSTORES

Ext. 3336

Listen to stories from some of our favorite bookshops in Colorado.

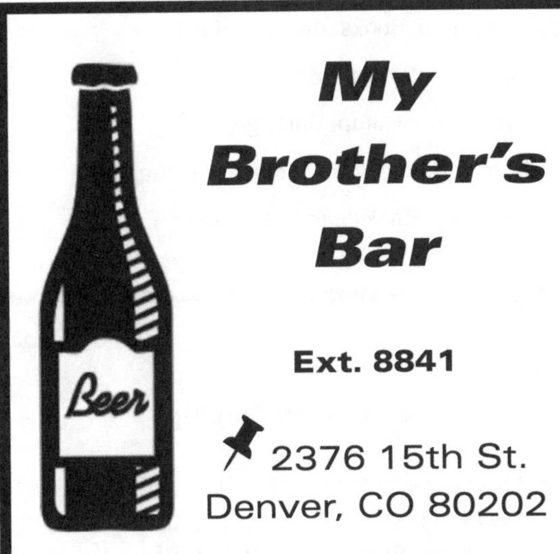

Beer
My Brother's Bar
Ext. 8841
2376 15th St.
Denver, CO 80202

COLORADO BOOKSTORES

- ❑ 32nd Avenue Books, Toys & Gifts: Denver
- ❑ A Folded Corner Inc.: Aurora
- ❑ Barbed Wire Books: Longmont
- ❑ Between the Covers Bookstore: Telluride
- ❑ Book Mine: Leadville
- ❑ BookBar: Denver
- ❑ Bookbinders Basalt: Basalt
- ❑ BOOKS in Cortez: Cortez
- ❑ Bookworm: Gunnison
- ❑ Boulder Book Store: Boulder
- ❑ Breck Books: Breckenridge
- ❑ Covered Treasures Bookstore: Monument
- ❑ Downtown Books & Coffee: Craig
- ❑ Explore Booksellers: Aspen
- ❑ Grand Valley Books: Grand Junction
- ❑ HearthFire Books and Treats: Evergreen
- ❑ Macdonald Bookshop: Estes Park
- ❑ MagWest Newsstands: Fort Collins
- ❑ Maria's Bookshop: Durango
- ❑ Narrow Gauge Book Cooperative: Alamosa
- ❑ Next Page Books and Nosh: Frisco
- ❑ Off the Beaten Path: Steamboat Springs
- ❑ Old Firehouse Books: Fort Collins
- ❑ Ouray Bookshop: Ouray
- ❑ Out West Books: Grand Junction
- ❑ Pacific Island Books: Thornton
- ❑ Poor Richard's: Colorado Springs
- ❑ Regis-N-Riley Books: Westminster
- ❑ Second Star to the Right: Denver
- ❑ Sudden Fiction: Castle Rock
- ❑ Tattered Cover: Denver, Littleton
- ❑ The Ahimsa Collective: Parker
- ❑ The Book Haven: Salida
- ❑ The Book Rack: Denver
- ❑ The Bookies Bookstore: Denver
- ❑ The Bookworm of Edwards: Edwards
- ❑ The Potter's House of Denver: Denver
- ❑ Townie Books: Crested Butte
- ❑ Turn a Page Book Shop: Aurora
- ❑ Welcome to the Bookstore: Brighton
- ❑ Who Else! Books: Denver
- ❑ Y.E.S.S. The Book Hutch: Durango

Community, Finding

Bear Town Community Center

Pickup hockey games for all ages!

For hours and info: 2943

We are the bears from Bear Town!

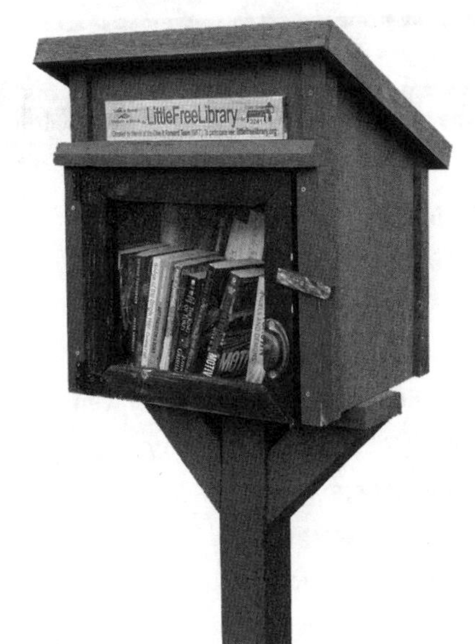

Ext. 7773

Connecticut

From the Mixed-Up Files of Mrs. Basil E. Frankweiler by E. L. Konigsburg 1024
The Baby-Sitters Club series by Ann M. Martin 5985

INTERVIEWS WITH CONNECTICUT BOOKSTORES

Ext. 8392

Listen to stories from some of our favorite bookshops in Connecticut.

Traveler Restaurant

Ext. 7126

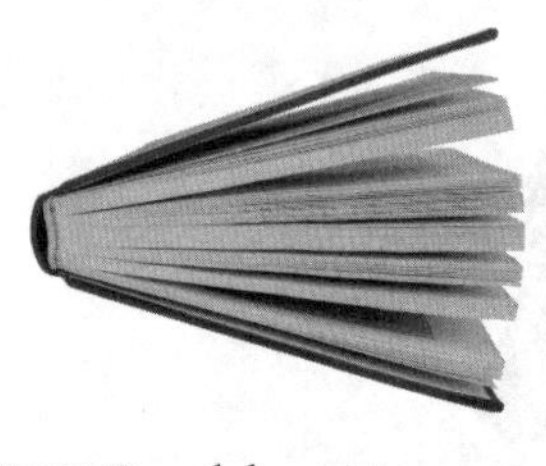

1257 Buckley Hwy. I-84
Union, CT 06076

Mark Twain House & Museum

Ext. 6964

351 Farmington Ave., Hartford, CT 06105

CONNECTICUT BOOKSTORES

- ❑ Awesome! Toys and Gifts: Stamford, Westport
- ❑ Bank Square Books: Mystic
- ❑ Barrett Bookstore: Darien
- ❑ Books on the Common: Ridgefield
- ❑ Breakwater Books: Guilford
- ❑ Burgundy Books: Old Saybrook
- ❑ Byrd's Books: Bethel
- ❑ Diane's Books of Greenwich: Greenwich
- ❑ Dogwood Books & Gifts: Christ Church: Greenwich
- ❑ Elm Street Books: New Canaan
- ❑ Harbor Books: Old Saybrook
- ❑ House of Books: Kent
- ❑ House of Books and Games: Windsor
- ❑ Lilly Street Books: Bridgeport
- ❑ People Get Ready Bookspace: New Haven
- ❑ River Bend Bookshop: Glastonbury
- ❑ RJ Julia Booksellers: Madison
- ❑ That Book Store: Wethersfield
- ❑ The Book Barn: Niantic
- ❑ The Book Colony: Meriden
- ❑ The Hickory Stick Bookshop: Washington Depot
- ❑ The Key Bookstore: Hartford
- ❑ Turning the Page: Monroe

Conservation

Ishmael by Daniel Quinn 6170
The Monkey Wrench Gang by Edward Abbey...........7559
Tracks by Robyn Davidson 3937
Who Stole My Religion? by Richard H. Schwartz 1952

Contagious Book Love

Atlantic by Simon Winchester.................................5984
Boy Meets Boy by David Levithan 3427
From the Mixed-Up Files of Mrs. Basil E. Frankweiler by E. L. Konigsburg 1024
Harry Potter and the Sorcerer's Stone by J. K. Rowling...8728

Brave and Kind Bookshop

Decatur, GA

Ext. 8333

An anonymous voicemail message about

Boy Meets Boy by David Levithan

Ext. 3427

The book I want to talk about is *Boy Meets Boy* by David Levithan. It's a typical story about two people falling in love, except those two people both happen to be male and the town they're in doesn't care that they're gay. It's just a love story. And it's still complicated and imperfect, tender and clever, hilarious and occasionally dark—but it's just a love story. As a straight person, I didn't realize how rare that was until I read *Boy Meets Boy*. There's a moment where Paul sings a song to Noah and the pronouns are all male. I found myself crying due to something so small, something I've taken for granted my whole life, that hit me the hardest. When I finished the book late at night, I messaged everyone I could find online. I needed to know if they'd read the book. If they hadn't, I would do whatever it took to get them a copy. I finally found a friend who responded in all caps. He said the book had gotten him through high school. And as we gushed and chatted, I was again humbled by a simple love story that's unapologetically gay. There's a part of me that wishes the title were less on the nose, because I want everyone to read the book, and I know there are many people who would fall in love with these characters if they didn't think it was just a "gay" book when they picked it up. But, I can see the power in a title like *Boy Meets Boy*. A book that doesn't assume it's unwanted or wrong just because it has gay characters. A book that celebrates this type of high school love in a way so many others do for people like me. A book that got my friend through high school. You should really read it, Ishmael. Thanks. ☎

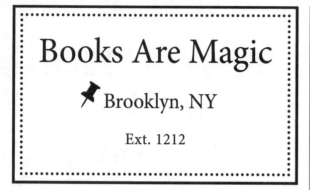

Books Are Magic

Brooklyn, NY

Ext. 1212

House of Leaves by Mark Z. Danielewski.................8733
I'm with the Band by Pamela Des Barres.................7739
On the Road by Jack Kerouac.................................5495
Redwall by Brian Jacques.......................................2803
The Art of Racing in the Rain by Garth Stein............7204
The Book Thief by Markus Zusak............................1060
The Brothers Karamazov by Fyodor Dostoyevsky 8631
The Chronicles of Narnia series by C. S. Lewis 3846
The Elements by Theodore Gray............................7203
The Great Gatsby by F. Scott Fitzgerald..................6865
The Martian Chronicles by Ray Bradbury 7549
The Power by Naomi Alderman 8895
Unbroken by Laura Hillenbrand.............................7578

Cooking

A Cook's Tour by Anthony Bourdain........................1642
Amelia Frump and Her Peanut Butter Loving, Overactive Imagination Is Cooking Up a Peanut Butter Storm by Debbie Roppolo........................2798
Fried Green Tomatoes at the Whistle Stop Cafe by Fannie Flagg 9715
Serious Pig by John Thorne....................................1114
Short Order Dad by Robert Rosenthal.....................1815

Courage

A Wrinkle in Time by Madeleine L'Engle.................2359
Cut by Patricia McCormick.....................................7810
Gilead by Marilynne Robinson................................8717
Into Thin Air by Jon Krakauer................................6747

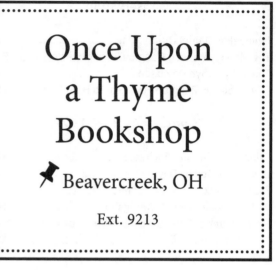

Once Upon a Thyme Bookshop

Beavercreek, OH

Ext. 9213

Call and tell us about your favorite cookbook.

774-325-0503

Ext. 2221

Just Listen by Sarah Dessen...................................7840
Speak by Laurie Halse Anderson 1372
The Book Thief by Markus Zusak.............................7953
The Golden Compass by Philip Pullman..................6863
The Tale of Despereaux by Kate DiCamillo...............6922
Wild by Cheryl Strayed 1953
Yes Please by Amy Poehler 3957

Creativity

Good Dog, Carl by Alexandra Day 8723
Steal Like an Artist by Austin Kleon 1825
The Art Spirit by Robert Henri 2356
The Catcher in the Rye by J. D. Salinger..................9667
What Do You Do with an Idea? by Kobi Yamada 1947

Crying

A Tale of Two Cities by Charles Dickens..................1021
Anna Karenina by Leo Tolstoy 4659
Blindness by José Saramago 8001
Crime and Punishment by Fyodor Dostoyevsky.......7550
Cutting for Stone by Abraham Verghese 6578
Extremely Loud and Incredibly Close by
Jonathan Safran Foer 8703
Redwall by Brian Jacques..2803
The Book Thief by Markus Zusak............................1022
The Middle Stories by Sheila Heti 9001
The Power by Naomi Alderman 8895

The Power of One by Bryce Courtenay.....................1043
The Storyteller by Jodi Picoult................................8912
When Breath Becomes Air by Paul Kalanithi 2367

An anonymous voicemail message about

A Tale of Two Cities by Charles Dickens

Ext. 1021

Hi, Ishmael. I wanted to talk about *A Tale of Two Cities* by Charles Dickens. I read it my freshman year of high school. Halfway through, I'll be honest, I was a little bored. The language was difficult to understand and it took a lot of focus—but I did read the whole thing and I didn't SparkNote it. I read the whole thing. By the end, the final two pages, I was crying, crying, crying. It was just so moving. The next morning, I knew we would have a quiz over the final reading in class, so I went to SparkNotes and read the summary of the final chapters, and I even felt myself tearing up reading the SparkNotes. So I had a great appreciation for the book. And then, my sophomore year of high school, this sweet blond-haired freshman boy let me know that he had received the copy that I had the previous year—and he knew this because, you know, in high school you write your name in the front of the book—so he had the copy that I had the previous year and he said he wanted to thank me because I had written a couple of notes in the margins and underlined things and . . . which is, you know, a nice gesture, a little odd. I found out later that he was sort of using that as an excuse to start talking to me, and I am so, so, so glad that he did. He's been my first love and I really hope he'll be my last. I've never really been a person who believes in things like fate. But the idea of Charles Dickens and *A Tale of Two Cities* bringing two people together is just too romantic a notion to ignore. I like our sappy story, just like I love that book. That's it. ☎

Dating

An anonymous voicemail message about

The Art of Fielding by Chad Harbach

Ext. 1006

Hey, Ishmael. I wanted to tell you a story about a book called *The Art of Fielding* by Chad Harbach, which has a lot to do with you and *Moby-Dick* in general. There's a professor in it who is obsessed with *Moby-Dick* and Herman Melville, but anyways, it's about baseball—and if you ask my dad, baseball is life. So it's also about life. My story is that I'm twenty-five, and I can pretty confidently say that I went on the best first date I have ever or will ever go on. I had gotten to know this guy for a couple of weeks before we went out. He knew I really loved to read, and he wasn't telling me where he was taking me for our first date. But after driving around in circles for a while, he ended up taking me to a bookstore. And I was like, "Um, you're taking me to a bookstore? Is there food involved? What is going on?" And he just kind of looked at me in the car, and said, "Well, I know you really love to read and I really like to read, too, so I was thinking that we could go in this bookstore and you could pick a book that you really want me to read and I could pick a book that I really want you to read and then we can switch and we can read those books." And so I ended up giving him *The Art of Fielding* and he gave me the biography of Augustus Caesar. Things didn't pan out with us, and that's okay because that was just kind of a gift. I got a book out of it and I got the best first date ever. And I got to give him that book which means so much to me. So thanks for listening. ☎

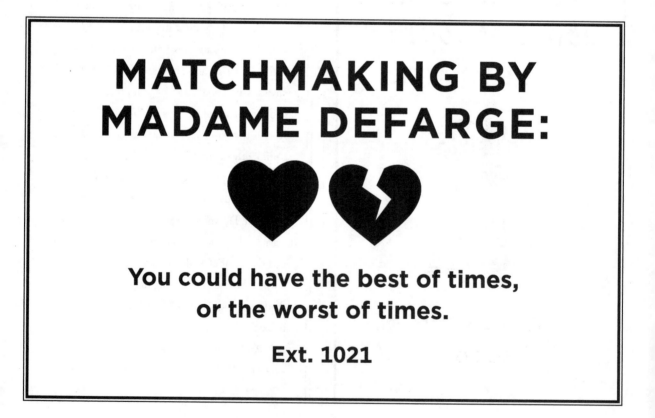

Jay's Flower Shop

We specialize in daisies.

Ext. 0250

MATCHMAKING BY MADAME DEFARGE:

You could have the best of times, or the worst of times.

Ext. 1021

Death

A Monster Calls by Patrick Ness..............................2646
Escaping the Giant Wave by Peg Kehret..................7696
Mortality by Christopher Hitchens..........................4000
Textbook Amy Krouse Rosenthal by Amy Krouse Rosenthal..2829
The Book Thief by Markus Zusak.............................1060
The Book Thief by Markus Zusak.............................2837
The Fault in Our Stars by John Green.......................4588
The Five People You Meet in Heaven by Mitch Albom 5853
The Stranger by Albert Camus 8911
Thirteen Reasons Why by Jay Asher 1004
When Breath Becomes Air by Paul Kalanithi 2367
Wintergirls by Laurie Halse Anderson......................7814

Delaware

Fight Club by Chuck Palahniuk................................9710

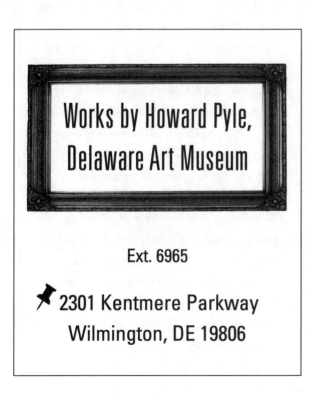

Works by Howard Pyle, Delaware Art Museum

Ext. 6965

2301 Kentmere Parkway
Wilmington, DE 19806

An anonymous voicemail message about

When Breath Becomes Air
by Paul Kalanithi

Ext. 2367

I knew I had to call, because last night I was sitting alone in the Sacramento airport quietly weeping after finishing Paul Kalanithi's *When Breath Becomes Air*. I can't ever remember having read such beautiful and heartfelt prose as he explores how to live a life of meaning, especially in the face of death. Like this message to his newborn daughter: "When you come to one of the many moments in life when you must give an account of yourself, provide a ledger of what you have been, and done, and meant to the world, do not, I pray, discount that you filled a dying man's days with a sated joy, a joy unknown to me in all my prior years, a joy that does not hunger for more and more, but rests, satisfied. In this time, right now, that is an enormous thing." His story took me back across eighteen years of time to a similar small hospital room where my mother, too, took her last straining breath. I was with her that night in a room that we filled with love, and as I told her that it was okay to go, I felt the last beat of her heart and then her breath became air, too. ☎

INTERVIEWS WITH DELAWARE BOOKSTORES

Ext. 5556

Listen to stories from some of our favorite bookshops in Delaware.

DELAWARE BOOKSTORES

- ❑ Acorn Books: Smyrna
- ❑ Bethany Beach Books: Bethany Beach
- ❑ Between Books 2.0: Arden
- ❑ Biblion: Lewes
- ❑ Browseabout Books: Rehoboth Beach
- ❑ GoGo Books: Newark
- ❑ Hockessin BookShelf: Hockessin
- ❑ MeJah Books, Inc.: Claymont

Depression

Cut by Patricia McCormick 7810
Everything, Everything by Nicola Yoon 8702
Furiously Happy by Jenny Lawson 8716
It's Kind of a Funny Story by Ned Vizzini 6750
Let's Pretend This Never Happened by Jenny Lawson..5760

An anonymous voicemail message about

What's Left of Me by Kat Zhang

Ext. 1949

Hi there, Ishmael. I received one of your calling cards from a girl in a bookstore, and I guess this is just me using that call. I just finished reading a book called *What's Left of Me* by Kat Zhang. It was a novel about this world where people are born into one body as two people, and eventually one of them fades away into nothing, leaving the other dominant and in control. One of the characters is the one that fades away, but she never is completely gone. She loses the ability to control the body, but she remains like a whisper to the rest of the world, unable to feel or speak. What I liked about the book is that it is uniquely redefining what it is to be human, and it fights to define what it is to be family. I think this book is a lot like a mirror, at least to my life. I know I have two very different sides to me. This, you know, happy-go-lucky part, and then this, just this depressed side of me that lurks in the shadow calling some of the shots. I guess neither will ever be completely gone from me. And I guess while I read the book, I just thought a lot about people and humanity and how we'll never really understand what's happening in someone's life because it's so easy to put on a mask. So yeah. Thanks for listening. Bye. ☎

Diaries

An anonymous voicemail message about

The Diary of a Young Girl by Anne Frank

Ext. 1929

Hi, Ishmael. Everyone knows the story of *The Diary of a Young Girl* by Anne Frank. But I read it in eighth grade and it changed who I am. After I read the book, I started to keep a journal—and I think I'm up to eight by now. It's not really like a laundry list of what I did today and what I'm going to do tomorrow. Instead, I fill it with quotes and little stories that I've started, and observations and everything that I can't say to people—mostly why I was so sad for so long. For a long time, I thought that I was collecting my life so that when I died my family would understand that I was sad, even though I have so much. I always had so much. But now I think that I'm recording for myself. Because now I know that I'm going to grow up. These journals aren't for my family to look back on when I'm dead, but for me to look back on when I'm older and to laugh at all the things that I thought were the end of the world and smile at the quotes that I remembered, and the horrible drawings. And I guess I have Anne Frank to thank for that. ☎

Disasters

Doing the Voices

BE THE VOICE OF ISHMAEL

Step 1: Call 774-325-0503.

Step 2: At the beep, instead of leaving a message about a book, say this phrase: "Hi, this is Ishmael. Leave me a message about a book you love."

Put your own unique spin on it and your voice could be featured in the outgoing message.

Driving

A Cook's Tour by Anthony Bourdain 1642
Ender's Game by Orson Scott Card 7695
The Grapes of Wrath by John Steinbeck 6864
The Middle Stories by Sheila Heti 9001
The Monkey Wrench Gang by
  Edward Abbey 7559
The Night Circus by Erin Morgenstern 4606
The Tenant of Wildfell Hall by Anne Brontë 6921
Tuesdays with Morrie by Mitch Albom 6000

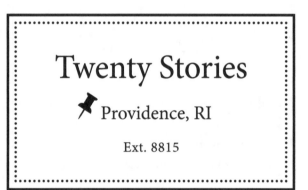

Twenty Stories

Providence, RI

Ext. 8815

"And all the great territories."

Ext. 3795

 To hear any of these stories, dial 774-325-0503 and dial the four-digit extension.

Westward Bound Trucking Co.

We leave the competition in the dust.

Organize with Tom: 6864

Dyslexia

Of Mice and Men by John Steinbeck........................3788
The Fixer by Bernard Malamud 6856

Empathy

Bridge to Terabithia by Katherine Paterson.............4959
Crazy Rich Asians by Kevin Kwan 5489
Do Androids Dream of Electric Sheep? by
Philip K. Dick 7687
Mockingbird by Kathryn Erskine 9328
Parable of the Sower by Octavia E. Butler 2799
The Bell Jar by Sylvia Plath......................................7577
The Reason I Jump by Naoki Higashida 9898
To Kill a Mockingbird by Harper Lee 6346
Wonder by R. J. Palacio 1954

Endings

City of Thieves by David Benioff..............................6681
Speak by Laurie Halse Anderson 1824
The Giver by Lois Lowry 6860
The Great Gatsby by F. Scott Fitzgerald 6866

The end:

"The drama's done. Why then here does any one step forth? Because one did survive the wreck."

Ext. 6543

An anonymous voicemail message about

Crazy Rich Asians by Kevin Kwan

Ext. 5489

A book I love is *Crazy Rich Asians.* I recently read it over summer break, at the suggestion of my roommate, who was born in Hong Kong, moved to Canada, and had told me so many stories about her family, the groups of friends that she had growing up, and what it was like to live as an Asian-born comedian. I found myself hearing her stories and her life through so many of the lines within the book, laughing and imagining the parties that they would go to and the gossip that they would share. For somebody who doesn't read fiction that often, I was pleasantly surprised that I couldn't put it down. I haven't seen the film yet but heard it's great. I would love to vote with my money and support more literature and Hollywood films of this nature, and I hope that my recommendation encourages somebody else to read it just like my roommate's recommendation got me hooked. Thanks. Bye. ☎

Equality

Bad Feminist by Roxane Gay 3481
I Am Malala by Malala Yousafzai 5987
Invisible Man by Ralph Ellison 1235
Parable of the Sower by Octavia E. Butler 2799
The Immortal Life of Henrietta Lacks by
Rebecca Skloot 4960
The Sneetches by Dr. Seuss....................................1042
To Kill a Mockingbird by Harper Lee 6346

An anonymous voicemail message about

The Sneetches by Dr. Seuss

Ext. 1042

The book I'm gonna tell you about, Ishmael, is *The Sneetches* by Dr. Seuss. I was born about five months before the U.S. Supreme Court ruled in *Brown v. Board of Education* that separate by definition is not equal. And in the years following that, we had Rosa Parks, the Montgomery Bus Boycott, Martin Luther King rising to prominence—and yet, when I started school six years later, our schools were still segregated. Race was of course a big topic. The question that I asked my white parents and at Sunday school and elsewhere was about race, and my Sunday school teacher told us, "White people are not better than colored people"—which was the politically correct term at the time—that "God wanted us to be separate just as crows and swans were. One was not better than the other, it's just that they were separate. And God made us different because we should be grouped differently." And I asked my Sunday school teacher, "What about hair color?" which really kinda seemed more to me like feathers than skin color, but he said, "Well, you'll understand when you get older." Of course, he was an adult, so I believed him. I would understand when I got older. That was just the way things were. The one thing that was more credible than adults was books, and my parents were very into books and it was the one thing that they would buy for us other than necessities, and other than on Christmas or birthdays. Dr. Seuss was and, in fact, still is my favorite writer. So, when his new book *The Sneetches* came out, my parents bought it for me. It's the story of star-bellied sneetches who think they're better than the sneetches who don't have stars on their bellies. This entrepreneur comes along and has a machine that will put stars on the bellies of the sneetches without stars, and the sneetches who originally have stars say, "Well, we know we're better, but now we can't tell the difference, so what are we gonna do?" And the entrepreneur, Sylvester McMonkey McBean, says, "Oh, I have a machine that will take stars off your bellies. You know stars are no longer stylish," and he charges them each to get stars taken off. The sneetches who originally were without stars say, "Oh my goodness, we need to be the same." So they pay McBean their money to have their stars taken off, going round and round until the sneetches no longer have any money. But, they figure out that no sneetches are better than other sneetches based on whether they have stars on their bellies or not. And of course I understood the racial implications of that, and it really made a profound difference in how I viewed civil rights growing up. Only as an adult did I think back about how it also was a nice metaphor for how there are certain people who profit either politically or economically from having races divided against each other. But in any case, it had a very profound effect on me as a young child. Thank you, Ishmael. ☎

Family

A Normal Pig by K-Fai Steele 2647
Chicken Soup, Chicken Soup by Pamela Mayer.......2222
Define "Normal" by Julie Anne Peters 9833
Everything Here Is Beautiful by Mira T. Lee 9767
Lace by Shirley Conran 7666
Long Live the Tribe of Fatherless Girls by T Kira Madden...5765
Looking for Alaska by John Green 9201
My Family and Other Animals by Gerald Durrell......7576
Persepolis by Marjane Satrapi................................1433
The Alchemist by Paulo Coelho...............................2362
The Friend by Sigrid Nunez....................................6857

An anonymous voicemail message about

The Namesake by Jhumpa Lahiri

Ext. 7886

Hey, Ishmael. When I first saw your project online, my first thought as a bookclubber was "Wow, I really want to take part in this, too." My second thought—which took me all of about two seconds—was that I wanted to speak about *The Namesake* by Jhumpa Lahiri. Though your mission is to share a story you've lived, there is no story that really strikes a chord in my heart like *The Namesake*. The book really follows two main stories. One of those stories is about a boy named Gogol. He's the child of Indian immigrant parents and grows up in this confusing space between two very different worlds. The first time I read this book, I associated so much with Gogol's world because it was my world. I understood his struggle to fit into two cultures and that search for an identity within these beautiful Indian traditions and this exciting American culture. It all really resonated in me. It was the first book that I felt captured the essence of me. Some time in college over winter break, I gave the book to my mom thinking, *You know, she might enjoy reading something that meant so much to me.* I remember coming downstairs one day and seeing tears streaming down my mom's face reading this book. To her, the story wasn't about Gogol. It was about the mother, this woman who immigrates to the United States with her husband after marriage. And she's just this strong woman who's left her family behind for her husband and her children. She leaves her India behind when she is young, although she always loved the country, and she adopts these American customs so her children will feel a part of the world that they chose. And she—my mom—read it in a way that I never had. She read it through the eyes of the immigrant mother who had embraced everything that was foreign to her for the people that she loved. And that just made me love this book so much more. It was no longer just my story. It was our story. My whole family's story. It was this testament to life of an Indian immigrant family. It captured that love for two countries in this beautiful poetic way. That's just why the book means so much to me and why I knew it was the book I wanted to share with you. Thanks so much. Bye. ☎

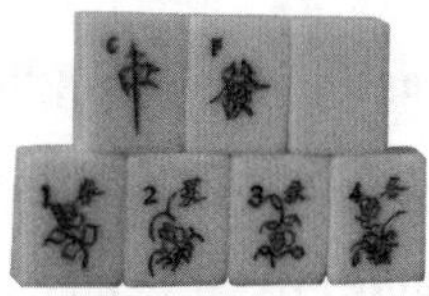

FAMILY FUN 'N GAMES

Play together. Stay together.

Chess • Bridge • Mahjong . . . and more!

Ask for Waverly: 7749

The Glass Menagerie by Tennessee Williams 6859
The House on Mango Street by Sandra Cisneros.....9325
The Joy Luck Club by Amy Tan 7749
The Namesake by Jhumpa Lahiri 7886
The Penderwicks series by Jeanne Birdsall 8893
The Stranger by Albert Camus 8911
The Things They Carried by Tim O'Brien 5720
Twilight by Stephenie Meyer 6668

Fathers

A River Runs Through It by Norman Maclean...........3648
A Tree Grows in Brooklyn by Betty Smith 1020
A Year Down Yonder by Richard Peck.......................3649
Long Live the Tribe of Fatherless Girls by
T Kira Madden...5765
Maus by Art Spiegelman...2506
Sabriel by Garth Nix 2805
The 13 Clocks by James Thurber 2831
The Alchemist by Paulo Coelho...............................9292
The Book Thief by Markus Zusak.............................2837
The Hobbit by J. R. R. Tolkien 1978
The Invention of Solitude by Paul Auster 2583
The Murder of Roger Ackroyd by Agatha Christie 9329
The World According to Garp by John Irving 1017
To Kill a Mockingbird by Harper Lee........................1013
Tuesdays with Morrie by Mitch Albom 6000

An anonymous voicemail message about

A Tree Grows in Brooklyn by Betty Smith

Ext. 1020

Hi, Ishmael, it's me. Today I want to talk to you about *A Tree Grows in Brooklyn* by Betty Smith. It's a classic girls' book and it follows Francie Nolan. Francie is the child of immigrants living in Brooklyn, and it's about how she grows up and what she loved about writing and reading. When I was fifteen, reading this getting ready to go to high school, it truly spoke to me because I love reading and I love writing and I was the granddaughter of immigrants. I loved it so much that I gave it to both of my parents to read. My mom read it and enjoyed it—'cause, like, mother-daughter reading, that's great—but my dad was always kind of like, "Okay, this is a girl book." But he read it and once he finished it, he said, "Hannah, I want to take you somewhere." So he took me to the cemetery where his aunt and grandparents were buried, and he walked me around the gravestones of the people I'd never met—my great-grandmother, my great-grandfather—and told me their stories about coming to the United States in 1911 . . . 1912 . . . 1915 . . . right about the time of Francie. He was telling me all these wonderful stories about my family that I'd never heard before. It was such a gift to be able to relate this book that I loved for many different reasons to a story that people I'd never known that were connected to me by blood and last name had lived. Now I just want everyone to read *A Tree Grows in Brooklyn* so that they can have that same connection to some part of their lives. Whether it's because they're related to immigrants or because they can have a moment of recognizing their family in the story, or recognizing what it's like to grow up. So I hope you get a chance to read it and I hope you have a great day. Bye. ☎

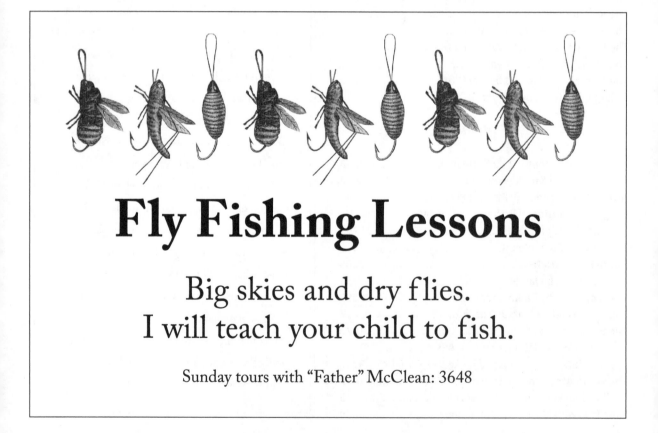

Fear

Dear America: Voyage on the Great Titanic by Ellen Emerson White 6684
Feed by Mira Grant 9324
Heckedy Peg by Audrey Wood 4621
Helter Skelter by Vincent Bugliosi 8730
House of Leaves by Mark Z. Danielewski 4625
Moby-Dick by Herman Melville 4627
Oh, the Places You'll Go! by Dr. Seuss 9836
Parable of the Sower by Octavia E. Butler 2799
Rosemary's Baby by Ira Levin 1808
Scary Stories to Tell in the Dark by Alvin Schwartz 1810
The Book Thief by Markus Zusak 7593
The Hot Zone by Richard Preston 6873
The Shining Girls by Lauren Beukes 9906
The Stranger by Albert Camus 8911
The Straw Men by Michael Marshall 7916

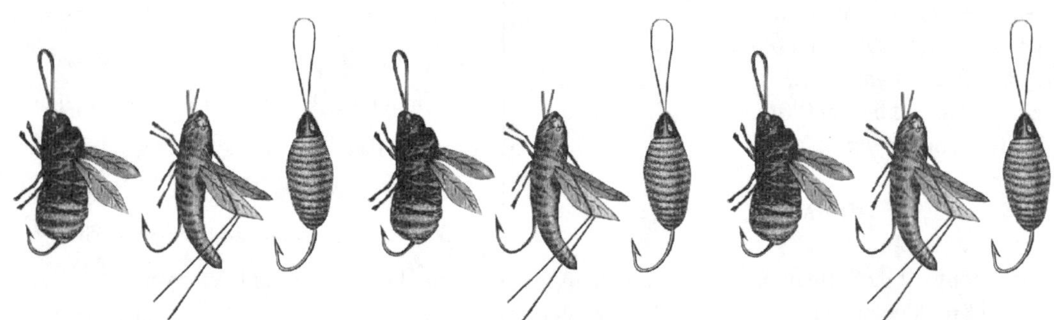

Fly Fishing Lessons

Big skies and dry flies.
I will teach your child to fish.

Sunday tours with "Father" McClean: 3648

 To hear any of these stories, dial 774-325-0503 and dial the four-digit extension.

Florida

Because of Winn-Dixie by Kate DiCamillo 1120
Dust Tracks on a Road by Zora Neale Hurston 7694
Florida by Lauren Groff 8772

FLORIDA BOOKSTORES

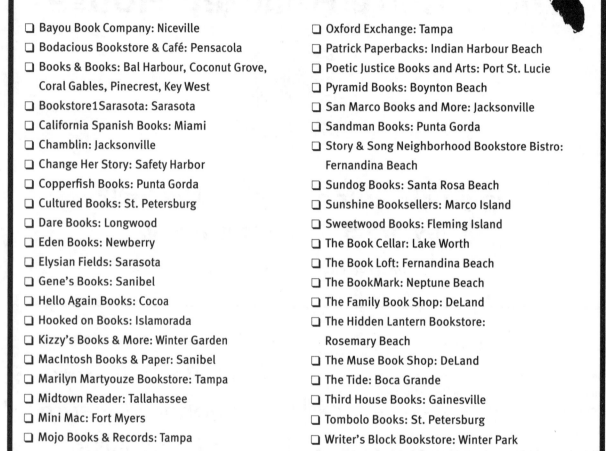

- ❑ Bayou Book Company: Niceville
- ❑ Bodacious Bookstore & Café: Pensacola
- ❑ Books & Books: Bal Harbour, Coconut Grove, Coral Gables, Pinecrest, Key West
- ❑ Bookstore1Sarasota: Sarasota
- ❑ California Spanish Books: Miami
- ❑ Chamblin: Jacksonville
- ❑ Change Her Story: Safety Harbor
- ❑ Copperfish Books: Punta Gorda
- ❑ Cultured Books: St. Petersburg
- ❑ Dare Books: Longwood
- ❑ Eden Books: Newberry
- ❑ Elysian Fields: Sarasota
- ❑ Gene's Books: Sanibel
- ❑ Hello Again Books: Cocoa
- ❑ Hooked on Books: Islamorada
- ❑ Kizzy's Books & More: Winter Garden
- ❑ MacIntosh Books & Paper: Sanibel
- ❑ Marilyn Martyouze Bookstore: Tampa
- ❑ Midtown Reader: Tallahassee
- ❑ Mini Mac: Fort Myers
- ❑ Mojo Books & Records: Tampa
- ❑ Oxford Exchange: Tampa
- ❑ Patrick Paperbacks: Indian Harbour Beach
- ❑ Poetic Justice Books and Arts: Port St. Lucie
- ❑ Pyramid Books: Boynton Beach
- ❑ San Marco Books and More: Jacksonville
- ❑ Sandman Books: Punta Gorda
- ❑ Story & Song Neighborhood Bookstore Bistro: Fernandina Beach
- ❑ Sundog Books: Santa Rosa Beach
- ❑ Sunshine Booksellers: Marco Island
- ❑ Sweetwood Books: Fleming Island
- ❑ The Book Cellar: Lake Worth
- ❑ The Book Loft: Fernandina Beach
- ❑ The BookMark: Neptune Beach
- ❑ The Family Book Shop: DeLand
- ❑ The Hidden Lantern Bookstore: Rosemary Beach
- ❑ The Muse Book Shop: DeLand
- ❑ The Tide: Boca Grande
- ❑ Third House Books: Gainesville
- ❑ Tombolo Books: St. Petersburg
- ❑ Writer's Block Bookstore: Winter Park

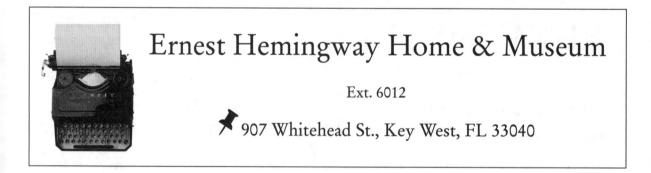

Ernest Hemingway Home & Museum

Ext. 6012

907 Whitehead St., Key West, FL 33040

Food

Starbuck's Coffee

Mornings without caffeine are blasphemous!

Ext. 7766

Sam's Organic Market

Eat your greens!

Call: 4614

Forgiveness

Crime and Punishment by Fyodor Dostoyevsky.......9835
Divergent by Veronica Roth..................................7686
Gilead by Marilynne Robinson...............................8717
Recovering from Reality by Alexis Haines................7676
Something Blue by Emily Giffin...............................7554

Friendship

Alice McKinley series by Phyllis Reynolds Naylor....3651
Beloved by Toni Morrison.......................................5668
Franny and Zooey by J. D. Salinger..........................9713
Good-bye, Chunky Rice by Craig Thompson............8720
I Am Malala by Malala Yousafzai.............................8734
Just Kids by Patti Smith...9841
Memoirs of an Imaginary Friend by Matthew Dicks...4775
My Ántonia by Willa Cather....................................9823
My Friend, the Vampire by Angela Sommer-Bodenburg...1036
Something Blue by Emily Giffin...............................7554
Something Borrowed by Emily Giffin.......................1820
Sula by Toni Morrison...1826
The Fan Man by William Kotzwinkle........................7556
The Fault in Our Stars by John Green.......................6751
The Phantom Tollbooth by Norton Juster.................7199
The Secret Garden by Frances Hodgson Burnett.....9903
The Sun Also Rises by Ernest Hemingway...............6919
The Time Traveler's Wife by Audrey Niffenegger..1044
Three Women by Lisa Taddeo.................................5929
Wonder by R. J. Palacio..1951

Georgia

Gone with the Wind by Margaret Mitchell...............8719
Simon vs. the Homo Sapiens Agenda by Becky Albertalli...2212
The Shining Girls by Lauren Beukes........................9906
The Underground Railroad by Colson Whitehead...2772

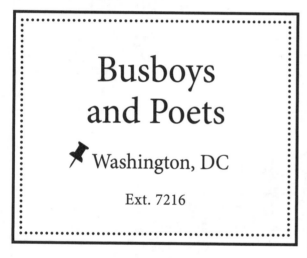

INTERVIEWS WITH GEORGIA BOOKSTORES

Ext. 3767

Listen to stories from some of our favorite bookshops in Georgia.

Bonaventure Cemetery

Ext. 6494

330 Bonaventure Rd.
Savannah, GA 31404

Alice Walker's Childhood Home

Wards Chapel Road
Eatonville, GA 31024

Ext. 6986

Georgia Writers Museum

Ext. 4487

109 S. Jefferson Ave.
Eatonton, GA 31024

GEORGIA BOOKSTORES

- ❑ 44th and 3rd Bookseller: Atlanta
- ❑ A Cappella Books: Atlanta
- ❑ A Novel Experience: Zebulon
- ❑ All Things Inspiration Giftique: Mableton
- ❑ Architectural Book Center: Atlanta
- ❑ [ash-ling] Booksellers: Toccoa
- ❑ Atlanta Vintage Books: Atlanta
- ❑ Avid Bookshop: Athens
- ❑ Book Exchange: Marietta
- ❑ Bookmiser: Marietta
- ❑ Brave + Kind Bookshop: Decatur
- ❑ Broad Street Books: Louisville
- ❑ Charis Books and More: Decatur
- ❑ Corner Bookstore: Winder
- ❑ Douglasville Books: Douglasville
- ❑ E. Shaver, Bookseller: Savannah
- ❑ Eagle Eye Book Shop: Decatur
- ❑ Enrichment Bookstore & Art Center, Inc.: Decatur
- ❑ Flipping Books and Stuff: Moreland
- ❑ For Keeps Books: Atlanta
- ❑ FoxTale Book Shoppe: Woodstock
- ❑ G. J. Ford Bookshop: St. Simons Island
- ❑ Gottwals Books: Byron, Macon, Perry, Warner Robins
- ❑ Half Price Books: Decatur, Marietta
- ❑ Hills & Hamlets Bookshop: Chattahoochee
- ❑ Horton's Books and Gifts: Carrollton
- ❑ Johns Creek Books & Gifts: Johns Creek
- ❑ Liberty Books: Lawrenceville
- ❑ Little Shop of Stories: Decatur
- ❑ Phoenix & Dragon Bookstore: Atlanta
- ❑ Posman Books at Ponce City Market: Atlanta
- ❑ Read It Again: Suwanee
- ❑ Righton Books: St. Simons Island
- ❑ SCAD Ex Libris Bookstore: Savannah
- ❑ Simply Books: Atlanta
- ❑ Southern Fried Books: Newnan
- ❑ Story on the Square: McDonough
- ❑ Tall Tales Books: Atlanta
- ❑ The Book House: Mableton
- ❑ The Book Tavern: Augusta
- ❑ The Book Worm Bookstore: Powder Springs
- ❑ The Bookshelf: Thomasville
- ❑ The Crazy Book Lady: Acworth
- ❑ The Listening Tree: Decatur
- ❑ The Story Shop: Monroe
- ❑ The Writer Workshop: Savannah
- ❑ Underground Books: Carrollton
- ❑ Walls of Books: East Ellijay

Ghosts

Gifts

An anonymous voicemail message about

The Alchemist by Paulo Coelho

Ext. 9292

Hi, Ishmael. A favorite book of mine is *The Alchemist*. I first came across it shortly after I had found out my father—who I hadn't spoken to in over ten years—had killed himself. I was trying to figure out what I was doing with my life. I'd been teaching, but it wasn't what I wanted to do forever. And I quit my job and went back to school, and I came across this book. It's this wonderful journey of a young man who travels and meets people and in the end comes back to exactly where he started from. It was exactly what I needed in my life. I try to read the book myself at least once a year to remind me who I am. Every person I know who is going through something in their life—marriage, graduation, divorce, maybe just a rough time—I buy them a copy of *The Alchemist* because it's one of the most influential books in my life. And I think it's done the same for many others. Thanks for letting me share. ☎

Grandparents

A Christmas Carol by Charles Dickens....................1641
A Tale of Two Cities by Charles Dickens..................1401
Brown Bear, Brown Bear, What Do You See? by Bill Martin Jr. 5675
Dinnertime by Jan Pieńkowski 4592
Green Eggs and Ham by Dr. Seuss 6028
Harry Potter series by J. K. Rowling........................8726
Homegoing by Yaa Gyasi.......................................7201
Jonathan Livingston Seagull by Richard Bach 1218
"Now Close the Windows" by Robert Frost.............3786
Tales of a Fourth Grade Nothing by Judy Blume.......8013
To Kill a Mockingbird by Harper Lee........................4933
Too-Loose the Chocolate Moose by Stewart Moskowitz 4590

An anonymous voicemail message about

***Brown Bear, Brown Bear, What Do You See?* by Bill Martin Jr.**

Ext. 5675

Hi, Ishmael. I wanted to talk to you not about a particular book, but a reading experience. I became a grandmother last year and I have the good fortune of being able to take care of my granddaughter twice a week every week. Some of my favorite parts of the day are when she brings me books. She sifts through this pile that we have on the coffee table, and sometimes she throws a few on the floor, looking for that particular one that she wants. Usually you have to have one in each hand, and she'll bring them to me, put them in my lap, and then reach up so that I can lift her into my lap so we can read. It's the best part of my day, and it's funny, as we go through them she likes to read them multiple times. So we flip through and I read the words and she turns the pages, and sometimes she turns them faster than I have finished the words on the page and we make a game out of it. And it makes her giggle, which makes me laugh, too. Some of her favorites these days are *Brown Bear, Brown Bear, What Do You See?*, going through all the different animals, and she thinks it's pretty funny if she can flip the page before I'm done reading. Another one she likes right now is called *A Curious Menagerie* and it's got these beautiful illustrations of groups of animals on the page. Most of her books are board books, but this one happens to be paper pages and she's so delicate as she turns them. And we look at the mischief of mice or the power of giraffes or a gaze of raccoons, and she just thinks it's the best, and I wish it could go on all day. So for now I'll read the words and she can turn the pages, and I know at some point—it's probably going to come quickly—that she'll be reading me stories, and I really look forward to that time. Just wanted to share that with you. Thanks. ☎

Gratitude

It's Kind of a Funny Story by Ned Vizzini 4597
Percy Jackson and the Olympians series by Rick Riordan 2801
Serious Pig by John Thorne...................................1114
Surviving the Angel of Death by Eva Mozes Kor and Lisa Rojany Buccieri 2364
Textbook Amy Krouse Rosenthal by Amy Krouse Rosenthal 2829

The Collected Schizophrenias by Esmé Weijun Wang....................9774
The Perks of Being a Wallflower by Stephen Chbosky....................7808
The Storyteller by Jodi Picoult....................8912
What Happens Next by Colleen Clayton....................7575

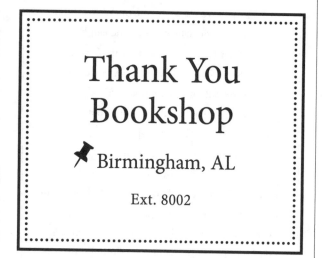

Thank You Bookshop

Birmingham, AL

Ext. 8002

Leave a message for an author you'd like to thank.

774-325-0503

Listen to messages of gratitude: 6738

Grief

American Gods by Neil Gaiman....................4656
Harry Potter series by J. K. Rowling....................8727
Invisible Cities by Italo Calvino....................7336
Misc by Anita Shreve....................4772
The Curious Charms of Arthur Pepper by Phaedra Patrick....................3845
The Razor's Edge by W. Somerset Maugham....................9401
White Oleander by Janet Fitch....................7572

An anonymous voicemail message about

Invisible Cities by Italo Calvino

Ext. 7336

I just finished reading *Invisible Cities* again by Italo Calvino. The book opened up to me in more ways than it has ever before. I picked at the folds and crevices, the reflections and the darkness from each journey to piece together my own version of my hometown, Lahore, in my mind's eye. I lost my last remaining grandparent two days past. Seven thousand two hundred and eighty-nine miles away from home, the only way I could find solace was to go to *Invisible Cities* in the hopes that I could reconnect with my dead grandmother. We shared a love of history, of cityscapes and memories, of poems and autumn trees, old photographs and family trees. I'm seven thousand two hundred and eighty-nine miles away from home and I can almost feel Lahore from her wise old eyes. I didn't get a chance to say goodbye to her in person. So here I am bidding you farewell. I miss you. ☎

Growing Up

32 Candles by Ernessa T. Carter 7553
A Series of Unfortunate Events by Lemony Snicket 7206
Escaping the Giant Wave by Peg Kehret 7696
Girl by Blake Nelson 8721
Harry Potter series by J. K. Rowling 7561
Invisible Man by Ralph Ellison 5348
Norwegian Wood by Haruki Murakami 3783
Sweetbitter by Stephanie Danler 1827
The Age of Miracles by Karen Thompson Walker 1948
The Catcher in the Rye by J. D. Salinger 6969
The Diary of a Young Girl by Anne Frank 1929
The Littles to the Rescue by John Peterson 6879
The Mozart Season by Virginia Euwer Wolff 7884
The Phantom Tollbooth by Norton Juster 8894

Grown-Ups

A Little Princess by Frances Hodgson Burnett 2644
It's Kind of a Funny Story by Ned Vizzini 6750
The Girl Who Owned a City by O. T. Nelson 4595
The Little Prince by Antoine de Saint-Exupéry 7777
The Phantom Tollbooth by Norton Juster 7199

Hard Books

Dune by Frank Herbert..7693
Infinite Jest by David Foster Wallace 6745
Moby-Dick by Herman Melville...............................4776
S. by J. J. Abrams and Doug Dorst 2804
Ulysses by James Joyce...3939

Hawaii

The Descendants by Kaui Hart Hemmings..............3441

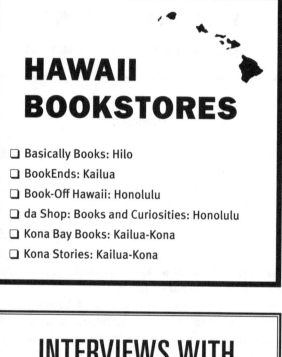

Diamond Head

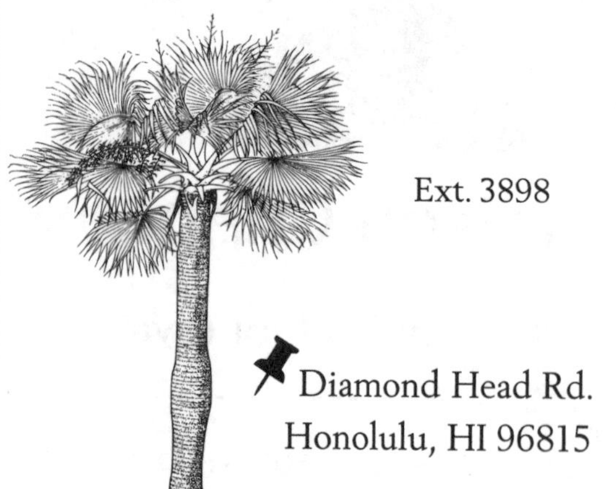

Ext. 3898

Diamond Head Rd.
Honolulu, HI 96815

HAWAII BOOKSTORES

- Basically Books: Hilo
- BookEnds: Kailua
- Book-Off Hawaii: Honolulu
- da Shop: Books and Curiosities: Honolulu
- Kona Bay Books: Kailua-Kona
- Kona Stories: Kailua-Kona

INTERVIEWS WITH HAWAII BOOKSTORES

Ext. 9733

Listen to stories from some of our favorite bookshops in Hawaii.

Health

Catch-22 by Joseph Heller 2244
Fear and Loathing in Las Vegas by Hunter S. Thompson 9709
Six Months to Live by Lurlene McDaniel....................7841
The Collected Stories of Isaac Bashevis Singer by Isaac Bashevis Singer 1012
The Fault in Our Stars by John Green........................2000
The Hot Zone by Richard Preston 6873
The Stranger by Albert Camus 8911
Unbearable Lightness by Portia de Rossi 7551
Wintergirls by Laurie Halse Anderson 7814

Heartbreak

A Cook's Tour by Anthony Bourdain 1642
Delirium by Lauren Oliver 6685
Full Moon O Sagashite by Arina Tanemura 9714
Love & Misadventure by Lang Leav 3001
Merriam-Webster's Collegiate Dictionary..................7041
Norwegian Wood by Haruki Murakami 3783

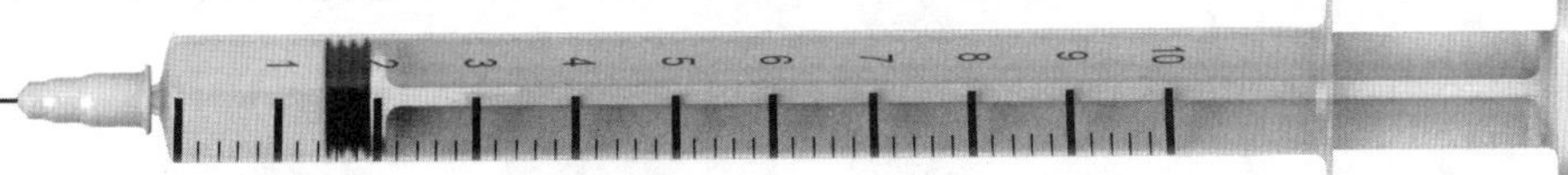

Heroes

 To hear any of these stories, dial 774-325-0503 and dial the four-digit extension.

Women's Clinic

Don't let the bastards grind you down

Ext. 6868

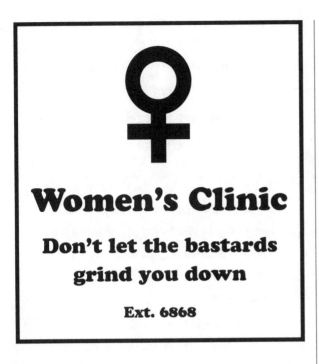

Harry Potter series by J. K. Rowling........................7561
I Know Why the Caged Bird Sings by Maya Angelou....7570
I Know Why the Caged Bird Sings by Maya Angelou....8737
I'm with the Band by Pamela Des Barres................7739
Just Kids by Patti Smith..9841
Just Mercy by Bryan Stevenson..............................5755
Percy Jackson and the Olympians series by
Rick Riordan..2801
Sabriel by Garth Nix..2805
Song of the Lioness quartet by Tamora Pierce.........1818
The Book Thief by Markus Zusak............................1007
The Book Thief by Markus Zusak............................7333
The Scarlet Letter by Nathaniel Hawthorne............9905
Where the Crawdads Sing by Delia Owens..............2945
Yes Please by Amy Poehler....................................3957

High School

A Tale of Two Cities by Charles Dickens..................1021
Do Androids Dream of Electric Sheep? by
Philip K. Dick...7688
Fear and Loathing in Las Vegas by Hunter S.
Thompson..9709
Horton Hears a Who! by Dr. Seuss..........................8732
Moby-Dick by Herman Melville..............................4627
The Giving Tree by Shel Silverstein.........................6861
The Maze Runner by James Dashner.......................6881
Thirteen Reasons Why by Jay Asher........................1052

History

Arabian Sands by Wilfred Thesiger.........................4660
Blood in the Water by Heather Ann Thompson........5670
City of Thieves by David Benioff.............................6681
Dear America: Voyage on the Great Titanic by Ellen
Emerson White...6684
First They Killed My Father by Loung Ung...............9712

Prom Rentals

Red-hot gowns! Firey tuxedos!

Message Carrie for fittings: 5676

History of Plymouth Plantation by William Bradford 1965
Just Mercy by Bryan Stevenson 5755
Maus by Art Spiegelman 2506
Michael Collins and the Troubles by Ulick O'Connor 7815
Persepolis by Marjane Satrapi 1433
Surviving the Angel of Death by Eva Mozes Kor and Lisa Rojany Buccieri 2036
The Boys in the Boat by Daniel James Brown 3844
The Diary of a Young Girl by Anne Frank 2035
The Professor and the Madman by Simon Winchester 8896
The Spirit of Fairhope by Dean and Megrez R. Mosher 8910
The Yellow Star by Carmen Agra Deedy 6923
Too Like the Lightning by Ada Palmer 3936

Holidays

A Christmas Carol by Charles Dickens 1019
A Christmas Carol by Charles Dickens 1641
Bridge to Terabithia by Katherine Paterson 4959
Eragon by Christopher Paolini 4602
Icy Sparks by Gwyn Hyman Rubio 7740
The Best Christmas Pageant Ever by Barbara Robinson 2836

Christmas Tree Farm

Ext. 1019

An anonymous voicemail message about

Maus
by Art Spiegelman

Ext. 2506

Hi, Ishmael. I read this book in the tenth grade called *Maus*, this man's story of going through World War II. It's all told by his son. I connected with it because my father was a Holocaust survivor. I remember giving him the book and saying, "Dad, does any of this stuff evoke any kind of emotion in you?" And he said, "Yeah." He told me that he vaguely remembered this man named Vladek, the man in the book, and seeing thousands of people die before his eyes. It broke me to a point where I thought that there are books that are written about people's tragic stories. People who are survivors. They bleed history. And it was profound that my father knew this man and knew his story. If you were to take every Holocaust survivor and write a book or make a graphic novel or make a movie about them, you would have this encyclopedia of every point of view that you could possibly have. I think it's quite amazing that we have these storytellers that are still alive. And I think we should treasure them to the greatest extent. ☎

An anonymous voicemail message about

The House on Mango Street by Sandra Cisneros

Ext. 8864

Hi, Ishmael. I'm Ellie. I want to talk to you about a book called *The House on Mango Street.* It's written by Sandra Cisneros and I love it to death. The main character, Esperanza, is a Latina just like I am. I can relate to a lot of things that happen in her household, and a lot of feelings that are shared by her and her family. I think it's really cool to see someone, a protagonist, especially who's similar to me. This girl doesn't have blond hair, blue eyes. She's like me. She has brown hair, brown eyes. She worries about her shoes and looking silly in front of her family. She has to dance with her uncle. I love it. I love the way the book is written. It's so poetic, it's beautiful. The passage where she says, "You can never have too much sky"—I look at the sky every day and I think that. I think it's great that Ms. Cisneros can come up and show us our own lives through something that she writes. And feelings of, you know, not knowing where you're gonna go, but knowing that you want to leave and then knowing that you have to come back. Because your roots are what bring you back. Even if you don't want them to. I love it because I finally know that I'm not alone and that that happens to other people, especially in my culture, too. I think it's just amazing. So, read *The House on Mango Street,* 'cause it's a beauty. Thanks. ☎

Home

Looking for Alaska by John Green 9201
Serious Pig by John Thorne.....................................1114
Speak by Laurie Halse Anderson 1824
The Chronicles of Narnia series by C. S. Lewis 3846
The Complete Stories by Flannery O'Connor 4848
The House on Mango Street by Sandra Cisneros.....8864
The Little Prince by Antoine de Saint-Exupéry.........7777
The Phantom Tollbooth by Norton Juster.................9099

Homesickness

A Christmas Carol by Charles Dickens.....................1641
A Little Princess by Frances Hodgson Burnett 7546
Invisible Cities by Italo Calvino 7336
Les Misérables by Victor Hugo...............................7552
Living Buddha, Living Christ by Thich Nhat Hanh 4587
The Complete Stories by Flannery O'Connor 4848
The Odyssey by Homer 7888

Hope

A Dog's Purpose by W. Bruce Cameron 3120
Define "Normal" by Julie Anne Peters 9833
Evicted by Matthew Desmond.................................9707
I Know Why the Caged Bird Sings by
Maya Angelou..8737
Ishmael by Daniel Quinn 1035

So Sad Today by Melissa Broder.............................9821
The Book Thief by Markus Zusak.............................7593
The Chronicles of Narnia series by C. S. Lewis 3846
The Diary of a Young Girl by Anne Frank..................4850

Hospitals

An anonymous voicemail message about

The Little Prince by Antoine de Saint-Exupéry

Ext. 3223

Early last year, I had a premature baby. He was born at twenty-five weeks, and due to some circumstances he actually weighed less than one pound. Soon after he was born, when I felt like there was nothing that I could do for this little baby that I had created that was fighting for his life every day, I decided to read him *The Little Prince*, because here he was, this little, little thing, and he was truly a little prince. I sat next to his incubator for days and just read this book to him. Those were beautiful moments. It's always been my number one thing in the whole world that if I can't do anything else, I just hope that I can always read books. And I read him *The Little Prince*, and when it was done, I really felt like we shared a special moment. Sadly, when he was eight months old, he passed away. I've really felt like this book just was him. He was the little prince in this book. He came to this earth and he was with us for eight months, and he taught us many lessons about love and life and strength and desire and will. Then, in the end, he just grew tired and he went back home. Back home to his star. Now, when I get sad, when I miss him more than I can even bear, I know that if I look up at the stars he's there with me. And there he is, looking at me and laughing with me, like it says in the book. And I can just remember him. Remember his beauty. Because like the stars, he's just as beautiful. ☎

Humanity

An anonymous voicemail message about

Speak
by Laurie Halse Anderson

Ext. 5998

My favorite novel is *Speak* by Laurie Halse Anderson. As someone who has been sexually assaulted, it helped me to cope with the trauma that I was facing. Today's rape culture is all about blame and accusation. *Is it the woman's fault? Is it the man's?* We are so hung up on blame that we fail to acknowledge the woman who just wants help. Maybe this is controversial of me to say, and maybe this will hurt someone's personal ideology, but during my sexual assault case everyone asked me, *What? Why? How? When? Who?* But nobody told me how to live with what happened to me. Melinda's thoughts in the novel and actions help me to cope. But, if I'm relying on fictional characters to help me more than people who have certified degrees, then that clearly shows the problem with today's world. We are stuck in our fictional worlds because the real one is too cold. When it comes to these cases, we shouldn't apply hostility. We should apply love and compassion. And while prevention is important, it's not worth the argument if you're just going to continue to personally victimize the woman. There's so much more than what society leads on. That is why *Speak* by Laurie Halse Anderson is my favorite book. And that's why it helps me to continue to live with my own story. ☎

The Nightingale by Kristin Hannah 7202
The Outsiders by S. E. Hinton 7337
The Perks of Being a Wallflower by Stephen Chbosky 7891
The Sirens of Titan by Kurt Vonnegut 8632
The Sneetches by Dr. Seuss 1042
The Strange and Beautiful Sorrows of Ava Lavender by Leslye Walton 7915
The Underground Railroad by Colson Whitehead 2772
The Yellow Star by Carmen Agra Deedy 6923
Their Eyes Were Watching God by Zora Neale Hurston 5927
Things the Grandchildren Should Know by Mark Oliver Everett 9330
This Blinding Absence of Light by Tahar Ben Jelloun 5928
Three Women by Lisa Taddeo 5929
Through Gates of Splendor by Elisabeth Elliot 4932
Us Against You by Fredrik Backman 2943
What's Left of Me by Kat Zhang 1949

Idaho

The Man Who Fell in Love with the Moon by Tom Spanbauer 1766

110-Year-Old Tree Little Free Library

Ext. 7723

716½ N. A St.
Coeur d'Alene, ID 83814

INTERVIEWS WITH IDAHO BOOKSTORES

Ext. 8739

Listen to stories from some of our favorite bookshops in Idaho.

Sun Valley Lodge,
Suite 206

Ext. 3266

1 Sun Valley Rd., Sun Valley, ID 83353

IDAHO BOOKSTORES

- ❑ AfriWare Books Co.: Maywood
- ❑ BookPeople of Moscow: Moscow
- ❑ Chapter One Bookstore: Ketchum
- ❑ Iconoclast Books & Gifts: Hailey
- ❑ Once and Future Books: Boise
- ❑ Rediscovered Books: Boise
- ❑ The Barn Owl Books and Gifts: McCall
- ❑ The Well-Read Moose: Coeur d'Alene
- ❑ VandalStore: Boise, Moscow
- ❑ Vanderford's Books and Office Products: Sandpoint

Illinois

Babe & Me by Dan Gutman 3353
Dandelion Wine by Ray Bradbury............................6683
Dandelion Wine by Ray Bradbury............................7571
The House on Mango Street by Sandra Cisneros.....6874
The House on Mango Street by Sandra Cisneros.....8864
Will Grayson, Will Grayson by John Green
and David Levithan 7332

INTERVIEWS WITH ILLINOIS BOOKSTORES

Ext. 4078

Listen to stories from some of our favorite bookshops in Illinois.

American Writers Museum

Ext. 5162

180 Michigan Ave., Chicago, IL 60601

 To hear any of these stories, dial 774-325-0503 and dial the four-digit extension.

ILLINOIS BOOKSTORES

- ❑ *play: Chicago
- ❑ 57th Street Books: Chicago
- ❑ A Book Above: Elmhurst
- ❑ Abraham Lincoln Book Shop: Chicago
- ❑ Afterwords Books: Edwardsville
- ❑ Anderson's Bookshop: Aurora, Downers Grove, Naperville
- ❑ Barbara's Bookstore: Burr Ridge, Chicago, Glenview, Vernon Hills
- ❑ Book Bin: Northbrook
- ❑ Booked: Evanston
- ❑ Bookends & Beginnings: Evanston
- ❑ Bookie's: Chicago, Homewood
- ❑ Books on First: Dixon
- ❑ Bookworks: Chicago
- ❑ Bound to Stay Bound Books: Jacksonville
- ❑ Cat & Mouse Games: Chicago
- ❑ Centuries & Sleuths Bookstore: Forest Park
- ❑ Chicago-Main Newsstand: Evanston
- ❑ City Lit Books: Chicago
- ❑ City News Café: Chicago
- ❑ Cornerstone Used Books: Villa Park
- ❑ Da Book Joint: Chicago
- ❑ Frugal Muse Books: Darien
- ❑ Half Price Books: Algonquin, Bloomingdale, Countryside, Downers Grove, Highland Park, Naperville, Niles, Orland Park, Schaumburg
- ❑ Hartfield Book Company: Monticello
- ❑ Harvey's Tales: Geneva
- ❑ I Know You Like a Book: Peoria Heights
- ❑ Jake's Place Books: Oak Park
- ❑ Jane Addams Book Shop: Champaign
- ❑ Kibbitznest Books, Brews & Blarney: Chicago
- ❑ King City Books: Mt. Vernon
- ❑ Kinokuniya: Arlington Heights
- ❑ Lake Forest Book Store: Lake Forest
- ❑ Lit. on Fire Used Books: Peoria
- ❑ Love's Sweet Arrow: Tinley Park
- ❑ Mindmosaic Books: Galesburg
- ❑ New Copperfield's Book Service: Macomb
- ❑ Open Books: Chicago
- ❑ Our Town Books: Jacksonville
- ❑ Page 1 Books: Evanston
- ❑ Pilsen Community Books: Chicago
- ❑ Prairie Fox Books: Ottawa
- ❑ Prairie Path Books: Wheaton
- ❑ Read Between the Lynes: Woodstock
- ❑ RoscoeBooks: Chicago
- ❑ Rosenblum's World of Judaica: Skokie
- ❑ Sandmeyer's Bookstore: Chicago
- ❑ Semicolon Bookstore & Gallery: Chicago
- ❑ The Book Cellar: Chicago
- ❑ The Book Nook: Peoria, Washington
- ❑ The Book Stall: Winnetka
- ❑ The Book Table: Oak Park
- ❑ The Book Vine for Children: McHenry
- ❑ The Bookstore of Glen Ellyn: Glen Ellyn
- ❑ The Dial Bookshop: Chicago
- ❑ The Sly Fox: Virden
- ❑ Town House Books & Cafe: Charles
- ❑ Unabridged Bookstore: Chicago
- ❑ Uncharted Books: Chicago
- ❑ Varia: Chicago
- ❑ Volumes Bookcafe: Chicago
- ❑ Wicker Park Secret Agent Supply Co.: Chicago
- ❑ Women & Children First: Chicago

Indiana

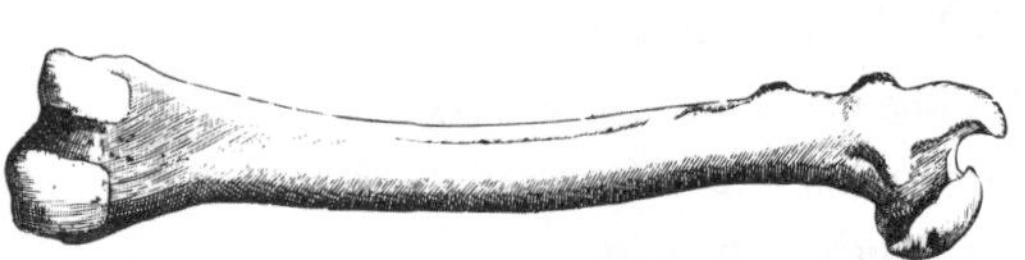

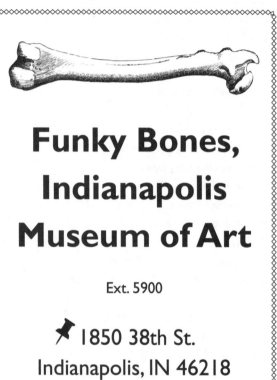

Funky Bones, Indianapolis Museum of Art

Ext. 5900

1850 38th St.
Indianapolis, IN 46218

Kurt Vonnegut Museum and Library

Ext. 7861

543 Indiana Ave.
Indianapolis, IN 46202

CENTER FOR RAY BRADBURY STUDIES

Ext. 1151

Cavanaugh Hall 121, 425 University Blvd.
Indianapolis, IN 46202

INDIANA BOOKSTORES

- ❑ 4 Kids Books & Toys: Zionsville
- ❑ AOM Bookshop: Indianapolis
- ❑ Austy's: Salem
- ❑ Basile History Market: Indianapolis
- ❑ Better World Books: Mishawaka
- ❑ Beyond Barcodes Bookstore: Kokomo
- ❑ Brain Lair Books: South Bend
- ❑ Brancamp Books: Batesville
- ❑ Destinations Booksellers: New Albany
- ❑ Eli's Books: Greencastle
- ❑ Fables and Fairy Tales: Martinsville
- ❑ Fables Books: Goshen
- ❑ Fallen Leaf Books: Nashville
- ❑ Friends of Art Bookshop: Bloomington
- ❑ Gwen's Book Mart: Evansville
- ❑ Half Price Books: Avon, Indianapolis, Fort Wayne, Greenbriar, Greenwood
- ❑ Indy Reads Books: Indianapolis
- ❑ Kids Ink Children's Bookstore: Indianapolis
- ❑ Main Street Books: Lafayette
- ❑ Newfields: Indianapolis
- ❑ Second Flight Books: Lafayette
- ❑ The Bookshelf: Batesville
- ❑ The Next Page Bookstore & More: Decatur
- ❑ Three Sisters Books & Gifts: Shelbyville
- ❑ Turn the Page: Westfield
- ❑ Viewpoint Books: Columbus
- ❑ Village Lights Bookstore: Madison
- ❑ Von's Book Shop: West Lafayette
- ❑ Wild Geese Bookshop: Franklin

INTERVIEWS WITH INDIANA BOOKSTORES

Ext. 4801

Listen to stories from some of our favorite bookshops in Indiana.

Inspiration

Americanah by Chimamanda Ngozi Adichie............4658
Bossypants by Tina Fey............1018
Dust Tracks on a Road by Zora Neale Hurston 7694
Hatchet by Gary Paulsen............7545
I Am Malala by Malala Yousafzai............8888
Just Kids by Patti Smith 6754
Life in Motion by Misty Copeland............5758
Recovering from Reality by Alexis Haines............7676
The Diary of a Young Girl by Anne Frank............2035
The Old Man and the Sea by Ernest Hemingway 5349
Wild by Cheryl Strayed 1953

Tina's Inspirational Posters

Ext. 1018

Iowa

A Thousand Acres by Jane Smiley 2113
Gilead by Marilynne Robinson 8717

INTERVIEWS WITH IOWA BOOKSTORES

Ext. 8802

Listen to stories from some of our favorite bookshops in Iowa.

Literary Walk

Ext. 4690

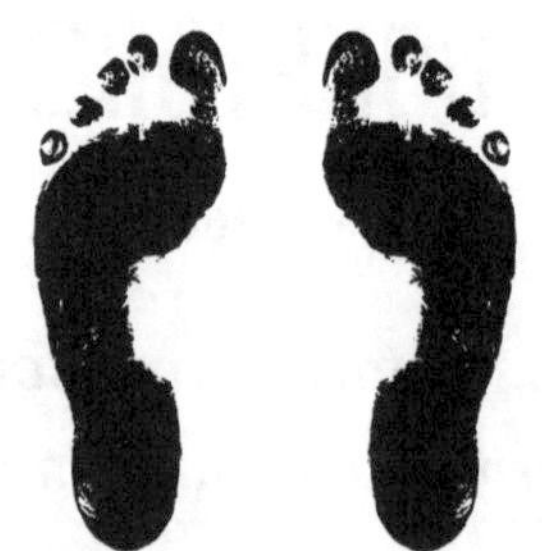

 To hear any of these stories, dial 774-325-0503 and dial the four-digit extension.

IOWA BOOKSTORES

- ❑ Alter Ego Comics: Marion
- ❑ Beaverdale Books: Des Moines
- ❑ Book People: Sioux City
- ❑ Book Vault: Oskaloosa
- ❑ Burlington by the Book: Burlington
- ❑ Dragonfly Books: Decorah
- ❑ Dudad's Hallmark Shop: Clinton
- ❑ Half Price Books: Cedar Rapids, Clive, Des Moines, Marion
- ❑ Hedgie's Books: Toys & More: Bedford
- ❑ Libélula Books: Waterloo
- ❑ M and M Bookstore: Cedar Rapids
- ❑ Master's Touch: Decorah
- ❑ Next Page Books: Cedar Rapids
- ❑ Pageturners Bookstore: Indianola
- ❑ Pioneer Bookshop: Grinnell
- ❑ Plain Talk Books & Coffee: Des Moines
- ❑ Prairie Lights Books: Iowa City
- ❑ River Lights Bookstore: Dubuque
- ❑ Sidekick Coffee & Books: University Heights
- ❑ The Book Rack: Davenport
- ❑ The Book Shoppe: Boone
- ❑ The Book Vine: Cherokee
- ❑ The BookWorm Bookstore & More: Bellevue
- ❑ The Haunted Bookshop: Iowa City
- ❑ The Learning Post Toys: Urbandale

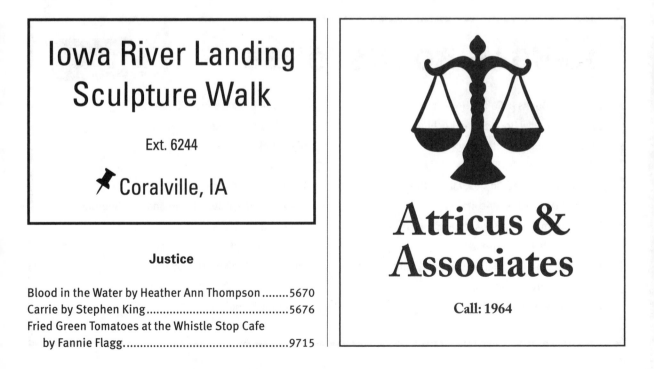

Justice

I Am Malala by Malala Yousafzai 8888
Just Mercy by Bryan Stevenson 5755
Sing, Unburied, Sing by Jesmyn Ward 3941
To Kill a Mockingbird by Harper Lee 1964

OZ MUSEUM

Ext. 6245

511 Lincoln Ave. Wamego, KS 66547

Kansas

Little House on the Prairie series by Laura Ingalls Wilder 5759
The Wonderful Wizard of Oz by L. Frank Baum......... 5926

INTERVIEWS WITH KANSAS BOOKSTORES

Ext. 4079

Listen to stories from some of our favorite bookshops in Kansas.

KANSAS BOOKSTORES

- ❑ Ad Astra Books & Coffee House: Salina
- ❑ Al's Old & New Book Store: Wichita
- ❑ Bluebird Books: Hutchinson
- ❑ Book-A-Holic: Wichita
- ❑ Claflin Books and Copies: Manhattan
- ❑ Eighth Day Books: Wichita
- ❑ Ellen Plumb's City Bookstore: Emporia
- ❑ Faith & Life Bookstore: Newton
- ❑ Half Price Books: Olathe, Overland Park
- ❑ Pioneers Press: Lansing
- ❑ Rainy Day Books: Fairway
- ❑ Rivendell Bookstore: Abilene
- ❑ Round Table Bookstore: Topeka
- ❑ Signs of Life: Lawrence
- ❑ The Book Barn: Leavenworth
- ❑ The Bookshelf: McPherson
- ❑ The Green Door Book Store and Gift Shoppe: Overland Park
- ❑ The Next Chapter Books and Novelties: El Dorado
- ❑ The Raven Book Store: Lawrence
- ❑ The Toy Store: Lawrence, Topeka
- ❑ Watermark Books & Café: Wichita

Kentucky

INTERVIEWS WITH KENTUCKY BOOKSTORES

Ext. 8803

Listen to stories from some of our favorite bookshops in Kentucky.

KENTUCKY BOOKSTORES

- ❑ A Reader's Corner: Louisville
- ❑ Blue Marble Books: Fort Thomas
- ❑ Carmichael's Bookstore: Louisville
- ❑ Carmichael's Kids: Louisville
- ❑ CoffeeTree Books: Morehead
- ❑ Half Price Books: Fayette Place, Florence, Lexington, Louisville
- ❑ Joseph-Beth Booksellers: Lexington
- ❑ Poor Richard's Books: Frankfort
- ❑ Robie Books: Berea
- ❑ Roebling Point Books & Coffee: Covington
- ❑ ShambroLa Books: Lexington
- ❑ The Cozy Corner: Whitesburg

Language

A Brief History of Seven Killings by Marlon James...1346
Homegoing by Yaa Gyasi...8731
Lolita by Vladimir Nabokov...5764
Merriam-Webster's Collegiate Dictionary...4445
Painted Horses by Malcolm Brooks...9825
Paradise Lost by John Milton...7569
The God of Small Things by Arundhati Roy...6862
The Great Gatsby by F. Scott Fitzgerald...6865
The People Look Like Flowers at Last by Charles Bukowski...7334

An anonymous voicemail message about

Homegoing
by Yaa Gyasi

Ext. 8731

Hey, Ishmael. Yaa Gyasi is the author of one of my favorite books, *Homegoing*. In 1619, the first enslaved people arrived in America, many from West Africa. 2019 was the year of return, where many African Americans returned to Ghana specifically to discover their roots and honor their ancestors. It was a bit of a homegoing. As a Ghanian native, I am grateful for historical fiction like *Homegoing* that walk us through the black journey of going from African to African American, and the stories of war, love, and identity that have shaped much of our culture today. *Homegoing* is a beautiful story about our difficult history. After reading it, many of my African American friends have said, "*Merek... î fie*," meaning "I am going home." Thanks, Ishmael. ☎

The Sun Also Rises by Ernest Hemingway...8913
Truth Serum by Bernard Cooper...4935
Ulysses by James Joyce...3939

LLÁMAME ISHMAEL.

Ext. 5088

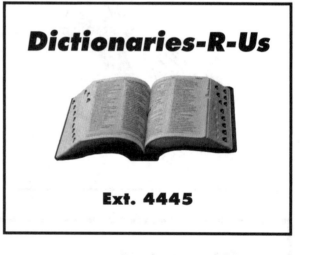

Dictionaries-R-Us

Ext. 4445

Laugh Out Loud

32 Candles by Ernessa T. Carter...7553
Bossypants by Tina Fey...1018
Catch-22 by Joseph Heller...5678
Fried Green Tomatoes at the Whistle Stop Cafe by Fannie Flagg...9715
Furiously Happy by Jenny Lawson...8716
Good Omens by Neil Gaiman and Terry Pratchett...1370
Great Comedians Talk About Comedy by Larry Wilde...1440
I'm a Stranger Here Myself by Bill Bryson...7738

Ford's Comedy Cellar

Closed Thursdays · Maximum Capacity: 42

For reservations, call Arthur: 1011

Let's Pretend This Never Happened by Jenny Lawson....5760
On Green Dolphin Street by Sebastian Faulks....3793
Sex Criminals by Matt Fraction and Chip Zdarsky....7838
Texfake by W. Thomas Taylor....1005
The Hitchhiker's Guide to the Galaxy by Douglas Adams....1011
The Regional Office Is Under Attack! by Manuel Gonzales....9901
The Sellout by Paul Beatty....9904
The Truth by Terry Pratchett....7557
We Are Never Meeting in Real Life by Samantha Irby....4832

Learning

Atlantic by Simon Winchester....5984
Evicted by Matthew Desmond....9707
Green Eggs and Ham by Dr. Seuss....6028
Hatchet by Gary Paulsen....7545
Huasipungo by Jorge Icaza....1669
I Know Why the Caged Bird Sings by Maya Angelou....7570
I Love You the Purplest by Barbara M. Joosse....1975
On Such a Full Sea by Chang-Rae Lee....5988
Tales of a Female Nomad by Rita Golden Gelman....2832
Tales of a Fourth Grade Nothing by Judy Blume....8013

An anonymous voicemail message about

Huasipungo by Jorge Icaza

Ext. 1669

Hey, Call Me Ishmael. The book I want to tell you about is called *Huasipungo* and this book was written by Jorge Icaza, who was an Ecuadorean writer. *Huasipungo* is a word in Kichwa that was used to refer to the small piece of land that was given to the Indians so they can use it for their own, but in exchange they have to work in a very abusive way toward the family's Spanish landowners. This book had a very big impact on me. I read it when I was twelve years old. I was looking for a book in my grandpa's bookshelf, and I found this super-old book there and it got my attention and I just started reading it. It shocked me, this story of abuse and conflict between indigenous people and Spanish people, and also people who have this mix between Indian and Spanish. The book was very, very hard for me. I was little and I didn't understand oppression. You don't really realize, and you don't get that information from your family or school. But the book was very explicit for me, and what I got at the end was this feeling of . . . that in the indigenous culture we have so many of these groups and it's so beautiful to see that, and see how groups survived a long period of time, of huge oppression and abuse. It's amazing. It's amazing how people just embrace their culture, and I felt part of it. Inside of me grew this desire to know more, because we're all part—we are all related in some way. Thank you. ☎

The Art of Learning by Josh Waitzkin 2833
The Power Broker by Robert A. Caro 9902
The Razor's Edge by W. Somerset Maugham 8897

Letters

13 Little Blue Envelopes by Maureen Johnson 3355
Griffin and Sabine trilogy by Nick Bantock 4594
Making Toast by Roger Rosenblatt 5768
The Perks of Being a Wallflower by Stephen Chbosky 7580
The Storied Life of A. J. Fikry by Gabrielle Zevin 7914

An anonymous voicemail message about

The Storied Life of A. J. Fikry
by Gabrielle Zevin

Ext. 7914

Hey, Ishmael. I'm calling to tell you about a gem of a book called *The Storied Life of A. J. Fikry* by Gabrielle Zevin. The main character, A.J., is a bookseller and a true bookworm just like me. He reads letters to his daughter and—paraphrasing one particular passage—he says, "The words you cannot find you borrow. We read to know we are not alone. We are not alone. My life is in these books. Read these and know my heart. We are not quite novels. We are not quite short stories. In the end we are collected works." Ishmael dear, everybody should read this book and remember that their own stories can be wondrous. I hope mine will be. So far it's looking good. So, to steal a line from A.J. one last time, "There ain't nobody in the world like book people." ☎

The Time Traveler's Wife by Audrey Niffenegger 1044
Words in Air by Elizabeth Bishop and Robert Lowell 2955

Librarians

13 Little Blue Envelopes by Maureen Johnson 3355
Belle Prater's Boy by Ruth White 4667
Gone with the Wind by Margaret Mitchell 8719
Harry Potter and the Sorcerer's Stone by J. K. Rowling..5347

We ♥ librarians.

Hear from one of our favorites: 8804

Are you a librarian? We'd love to feature you! Say hello at ishmael@callmeishmael.com

An anonymous voicemail message about

13 Little Blue Envelopes by Maureen Johnson

Ext. 3355

This is Miss Clark. I'm a school librarian, and when I remember moments in my life, I'll often associate them with books. When I was thirty-five years old, I was promoted to be the teen librarian at the public library where I worked. This terrified me, since it had been years since I'd read a teen book and I was sure that my recommendations would suck. I decided to visit a well-known teen librarian named Debbie Taylor to ask for advice. She was rumored to have psychic abilities that match people with books. When I met her, the first thing she did was comment on my ring, which I told her I had gotten in Egypt. We proceeded to have a lovely conversation about backpacking, surviving on twenty dollars a day, street food—everything but books. Suddenly, she excused herself and came back with a book called *13 Little Blue Envelopes* by Maureen Johnson, and said, "You'll see yourself in this book. Have fun on your European scavenger hunt." The book is about seventeen-year-old Ginny, a quiet New Jersey teen who gets a letter in a blue envelope from her adventurous, recently deceased aunt that contains one thousand dollars, a one-way ticket to London, and directions on how to find the other twelve envelopes. Ginny ends up traveling all over Europe, following the instructions of each letter, leading her to people and kooky situations she never imagined. I did see myself in the book: the intrepid teen who took a gap year and traveled to the Philippines, Israel, Egypt, Belgium, and the Netherlands. I'm still mastering my ability to connect teens with books, but I'll always associate *13 Little Blue Envelopes* with the moment I started working with adolescents and the beginning of my romance with young adult literature. ☎

I'm a Stranger Here Myself by Bill Bryson 7738
The Curious Charms of Arthur Pepper by Phaedra Patrick 3845
The Regional Office Is Under Attack! by Manuel Gonzales 9901

Libraries

Breakfast at Tiffany's by Truman Capote 4607
Moby-Dick by Herman Melville...............3780
Narcissus and Goldmund by Hermann Hesse...............3785
Pride and Prejudice by Jane Austen 4632
The Bell Jar by Sylvia Plath...............9832
The Library Book by Susan Orlean 4444
The Paper Menagerie and Other Stories by Ken Liu 7890
Where the Stars Still Shine by Trish Doller...............1301
Will Grayson, Will Grayson by John Green and David Levithan 7332

Life Changers

Downwind from Nobody by Joan Wells...............7692
Ishmael by Daniel Quinn 6748
Prep by Curtis Sittenfeld...............1050

In a rut? Find the book that can help you make a change:

For career troubles: Dial 7661

For friendship issues: Dial 7862

For love woes: Dial 2766

She's Come Undone by Wally Lamb 1813
The Brothers Karamazov by Fyodor Dostoyevsky 8631
The Fault in Our Stars by John Green.......................2000
The Golden Compass by Philip Pullman 6863
The Handmaid's Tale by Margaret Atwood 6868
The Hitchhiker's Guide to the Galaxy by Douglas Adams...1011
The Hitchhiker's Guide to the Galaxy by Douglas Adams...4242
The Stranger by Albert Camus 4626
The Truth by Terry Pratchett 7557
Thirteen Reasons Why by Jay Asher 4930
Through Gates of Splendor by Elisabeth Elliot 4932
Tiny Beautiful Things by Cheryl Strayed..................6059
White Oleander by Janet Fitch................................4001
Women Who Run with the Wolves by Clarissa Pinkola Estés 1640

Life Lessons

A Series of Unfortunate Events by Lemony Snicket 5000
A Series of Unfortunate Events by Lemony Snicket 8635
Babylon Revisited by F. Scott Fitzgerald..................4664
Cassandra at the Wedding by Dorothy Baker 3323
Infinite Jest by David Foster Wallace 9826
Love Does by Bob Goff..5767
Mockingbird by Kathryn Erskine 9328
Norwegian Wood by Haruki Murakami 3783
Oh, the Places You'll Go! by Dr. Seuss.....................9824
Recovering from Reality by Alexis Haines................7676
The Diary of a Young Girl by Anne Frank..................2035
The Giving Tree by Shel Silverstein 6861
The Glass Bead Game by Hermann Hesse 7818
The Scarlet Letter by Nathaniel Hawthorne.............9905
To Kill a Mockingbird by Harper Lee........................4933
Tuesdays with Morrie by Mitch Albom 6000

Loneliness

A Series of Unfortunate Events by Lemony Snicket....5000
Anthem by Ayn Rand 9326
Captain Underpants series by Dav Pilkey................6026
Let the Great World Spin by Colum McCann 9501
Siddhartha by Hermann Hesse 3814
The Complete Sherlock Holmes by Sir Arthur Conan Doyle 4603
The Particular Sadness of Lemon Cake by Aimee Bender..7889
The Perks of Being a Wallflower by Stephen Chbosky 7807

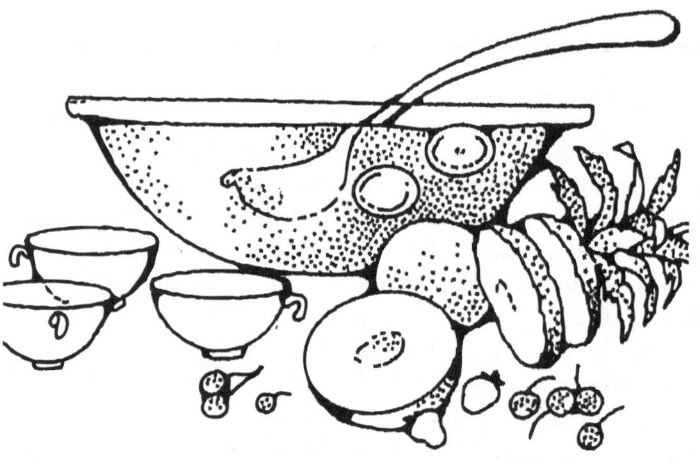

The Phantom Tollbooth by Norton Juster.................9099
White Oleander by Janet Fitch...............................4001

Long Books

American Psycho by Bret Easton Ellis 4657
Divergent by Veronica Roth....................................7686
Full Moon O Sagashite by Arina Tanemura..............9714
Inkheart trilogy by Cornelia Funke 8680
Moby-Dick by Herman Melville...............................4776
Unbroken by Laura Hillenbrand 7578
Women Who Run with the Wolves by
Clarissa Pinkola Estés.......................................1640

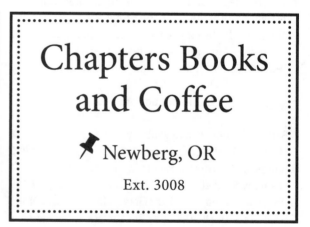

Loss

An anonymous voicemail message about

Wave
by Sonali Deraniyagala

Ext. 2944

Hi, Ishmael. I'm calling to talk about the book titled *Wave* by Sonali Deraniyagala. This isn't the book I had wanted to talk about. I'm an English teacher who studied literature in grad school, and I wanted to talk about a book with universal themes and sweeping motifs and rich symbolism. But that's not the book that . . . that has touched me in this way. That has haunted me and that I hold like a fragile candle of hope. This book is slim and often stark. It's hard to recommend because it's such a difficult read. It's the story of a woman who loses everything and everyone who matters to her in the 2004 tsunami that struck Sri Lanka. She was visiting family with her husband and her two young sons, and she lost all of them—her parents, too—when the Indian Ocean came and swept them literally out of her reach. This is her story. And it's so hard to read for anyone, but especially for me because I have a son who at the age of four was diagnosed with a genetic disorder that will take his life probably by the time he's twenty to twenty-five—or maybe he'll be one of the lucky ones who makes it to thirty. He's fifteen now, and I don't know when it will come. But I do know that at some point I'm going to watch my son die young, be swept from my arms no matter how hard I try to hold. He will be swept out to sea and I'll have to watch. I've wondered ever since his diagnosis eleven years ago what comes on the other side of that. What the author of this book shows me is that it's never going to be okay again, but that healing will happen. When she first lost her family, she went totally mad, and that I expect because I've already been there and I haven't even lost my son yet. But what surprised me was what came after the madness: the slow, slow climbing back to a life. And what maybe was disappointing but also powerful was that she never made it back to . . . I don't know. It wasn't a shiny new self-healing, where she woke up one day and everything was glorious again. It was never like that and it never will be like that when you lose everything. But she has something now. She has a broken life, but a true life. And I guess that's what I cling to. I think, *Well, I may never be whole again after losing the person that I love more than life.* But she survived and I will survive and there will be healing on the other side. This isn't the book I wanted to talk about, but I guess this is the book I need to talk about, and that I need to hold on to that hope and know that through it all we all come out on the other side stronger than we ever thought we needed to be or really should have to be. And that's all. Thanks.

The Bell Jar by Sylvia Plath....................................9832
The End of Your Life Book Club by Will Schwalbe.....1123
The Fault in Our Stars by John Green.......................6751
The Invention of Solitude by Paul Auster 2583
The Little Prince by Antoine de Saint-Exupéry.........3223
The Time Traveler's Wife by Audrey Niffenegger......1044
Tiger Eyes by Judy Blume.......................................3046
Wave by Sonali Deraniyagala..................................2944

Lost & Found

A Little Princess by Frances Hodgson Burnett 7546
A Supposedly Fun Thing I'll Never Do Again by David Foster Wallace..1963
Around the World with Auntie Mame by Patrick Dennis..4628
Assassin's Apprentice by Robin Hobb.....................4663

Belle Prater's Boy by Ruth White.............................4667
Blankets by Craig Thompson 3018
Girl by Blake Nelson 8721
Inside the Walls of Troy by Clemence McLaren 7547

An anonymous voicemail message about

Jonathan Livingston Seagull by Richard Bach

Ext. 1218

Hi. My name is Chelsea, and when I was about fifteen years old, my grandmother had a stroke. She had to be moved so that she could be taken care of by my family, and my mom and I went to her ranch in California to clear out her stuff. She had a lot of really cool T-shirts from the sixties and seventies, and I found one with a picture of a seagull on it and the word "Jonathan." I thought it was so mysterious. I asked my mom what it was and she told me that it was a T-shirt representing the book *Jonathan Livingston Seagull*. My grandmother's favorite book. I kept the T-shirt and I wore it all through the rest of high school. I still have it, and I really have always liked that T-shirt. A few years ago, my grandmother passed away while I was traveling through Italy for a month. I was unable to go to the funeral because I was in the middle of this trip, but the very next day I took the train to Venice, and I was walking around with my friend, who wanted to stop into a small little bookstore because she wanted to find a book about Michael Jackson, who had just passed away. I was looking around for books in English, and there was one small little bookshelf with books in English on it. My eye was immediately drawn to this little tiny blue spine of a book, and I didn't see what it was, but I pulled it off the shelf to have a look at it and it was *Jonathan Livingston Seagull*. This was a book that I had never seen before at a bookshop, so my breath was kind of taken away. I don't usually believe in signs from the afterlife or anything like that, but I had to buy this book. I didn't have any idea what it was about, actually. I certainly didn't think it was actually about a seagull, but it is. It's a fable about transgressing death and moving on to something greater. I never really knew my grandmother that well. It's only since she passed that I've learned a lot more about her, and I've learned that we have a lot in common—our love of literature, for one. I had no idea that my grandmother had been an English major and a poet. I myself am an English major and an aspiring writer. I also found out that she struggled with depression, which is something that I've struggled with as well. It just brings all the more meaning to this amazing thing that happened, finding this book on this small little bookshelf in this small little shop in Venice the day after my grandmother passed away. I still don't know if I believe in messages from the afterlife, but to me this event had so much meaning in it that I couldn't just think it was a coincidence. ☎

Louisiana

Carousel Bar

Ext. 9731

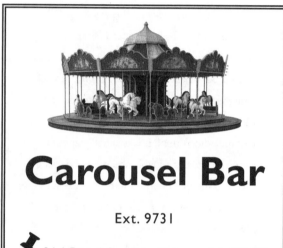

214 Royal St. New Orleans, LA 70130

Love

INTERVIEWS WITH LOUISIANA BOOKSTORES

Ext. 7672

Listen to stories from some of our favorite bookshops in Louisiana.

LOUISIANA BOOKSTORES

- ❑ Between the Lines Bookstore: Baton Rouge, Zachary
- ❑ Blue Cypress Books: New Orleans
- ❑ Cavalier House Books: Denham Springs
- ❑ Faulkner House Books: New Orleans
- ❑ Garden District Book Shop: New Orleans
- ❑ Kitchen Witch: New Orleans
- ❑ Looziana Book Company: Denham Springs
- ❑ Number 9 Books and Records: Ruston
- ❑ Octavia Books: New Orleans
- ❑ The Catholic Book Store: New Orleans
- ❑ The Conundrum: St. Francisville
- ❑ Tubby and Coo's Mid-City Book Shop: New Orleans

 To hear any of these stories, dial 774-325-0503 and dial the four-digit extension.

Galatoire's Restaurant

Ext. 4335

 209 Bourbon St. New Orleans, LA 70130

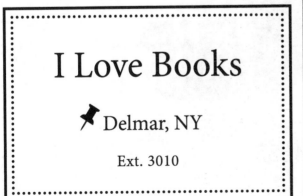

Love Does by Bob Goff 5767
My Ántonia by Willa Cather 9823
Not Even Wrong by Paul Collins.................................6802
The History of Love by Nicole Krauss.........................4343
The Neverending Story by Michael Ende 7568
The Velveteen Rabbit by Margery Williams..................6920
True Story, Swear to God by Tom Beland....................5494

Love Stories

Americanah by Chimamanda Ngozi Adichie............4658
Boy Meets Boy by David Levithan 3427
Franny and Zooey by J. D. Salinger..........................9713
Keeping You a Secret by Julie Anne Peters 8630
Pride and Prejudice by Jane Austen 4632

I Love Books

 Delmar, NY

Ext. 3010

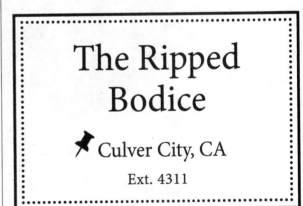

The Ripped Bodice

Culver City, CA

Ext. 4311

Mr. Bingley's Chocolatiers

It is a truth universally acknowledged that a single man in possession of a good fortune must be in want of the world's finest chocolate.

Ext. 4632

An anonymous voicemail message about

Keeping You a Secret
by Julie Anne Peters

Ext. 8630

Hi. A book I really love is *Keeping You a Secret* by Julie Anne Peters. Pretty extraordinary. It's about these two girls that fall in love, and a bunch of tragedy ensues, but it's also really happy and cheesy and mushy and gooey and trashy at times. It's like any other romantic type of story. It made my love sound human and not like news, you know? You hear so much about gay love stories being news and politics and all this controversy, and it was great to just have it be a story that was very human and very real. It made me feel better about myself and the love that I hope to find in life. It made me love my love as more than just some coming-out story. It made me feel fantastic, honestly. And for that I love this book so, so much. Yeah. That's . . . that's it. Bye. ☎

Paul and Noah's Wedding Cakes

Our commitment to quality takes the cake.

Call: 3427

Thomas Hill Standpipe

Ext. 4500

 41 Thomas Hill Rd., Bangor, ME 04401

Maine

MAINE BOOKSTORES

- ❑ Blue Hill Books: Blue Hill
- ❑ Bogan Books: Fort Kent
- ❑ Book Review: Falmouth
- ❑ BookStacks: Bucksport
- ❑ Bull Moose: Bangor, Brunswick, Lewiston, North Windham, Portland, Sanford, Scarborough, South Portland, Waterville
- ❑ Children's Book Cellar: Waterville
- ❑ Compass Rose Books: Castine
- ❑ Devaney, Doak & Garrett Booksellers: Farmington
- ❑ Fine Print Booksellers: Kennebunkport
- ❑ Hello Hello Books: Rockland
- ❑ Kelly's Books to Go: South Portland
- ❑ Letterpress Books: Portland
- ❑ Longfellow Books: Portland
- ❑ Main(e) Point Books: Islesboro
- ❑ Michelle Rice Sarma: Bookseller: Auburn
- ❑ Mystery Cove Book Shop: Hulls Cove
- ❑ Bar Harbor Book Shop: Bar Harbor
- ❑ Owl & Turtle Bookshop Café: Camden
- ❑ Print: A Bookstore: Portland
- ❑ Royal River Books: Yarmouth
- ❑ Sherman's Books & Stationery: Bar Harbor, Boothbay Harbor, Camden, Damariscotta, Freeport, Portland
- ❑ The Book Burrow: Kennebunk
- ❑ The Briar Patch: Bangor
- ❑ The Mustard Seed Bookstore: Bath
- ❑ The Tribune: Norway
- ❑ Treehouse Toys: Portland

INTERVIEWS WITH MAINE BOOKSTORES

Ext. 5089

Listen to stories from some of our favorite bookshops in Maine.

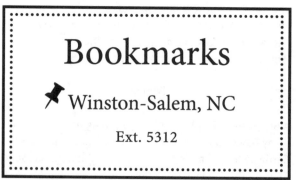

Marginalia

A Tale of Two Cities by Charles Dickens....................1021
Moby-Dick by Herman Melville...............................2112

Bookmarks

Ext. 5312

 To hear any of these stories, dial 774-325-0503 and dial the four-digit extension.

The Descendants by Kaui Hart Hemmings...............3441
The Great Gatsby by F. Scott Fitzgerald...................6867
The Secret History by Donna Tartt...........................9768
Women Who Run with the Wolves by
Clarissa Pinkola Estés.......................................1640

Marriage

American Wife by Curtis Sittenfeld.........................7562
Forever, Interrupted by Taylor Jenkins Reid.............6746
Stag's Leap by Sharon Olds...................................1822
The Year of Magical Thinking by Joan Didion...........5925
This Is Where I Leave You by Jonathan Tropper........8305
True Story, Swear to God by Tom Beland................5494

Maryland

The Immortal Life of Henrietta Lacks by
Rebecca Skloot...4960

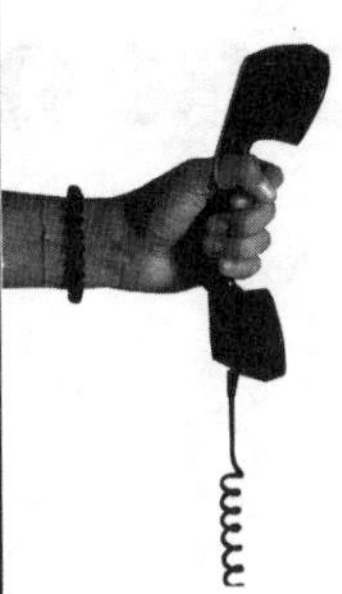

For as long as you both shall read.

Leave a message about the literature you used for readings at your wedding.

774-325-0503 Ext. 3768

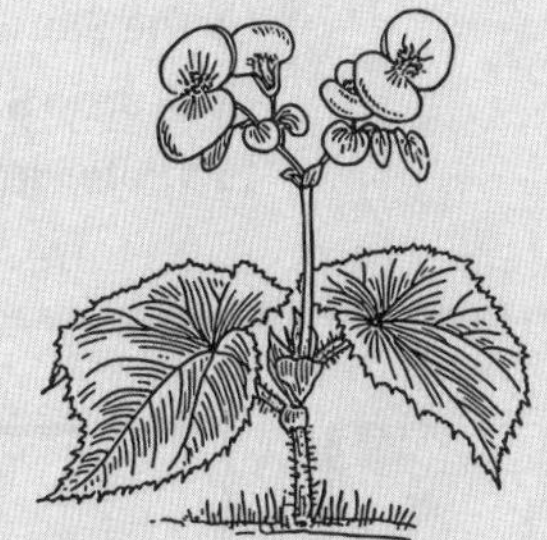

Dorothy Parker Memorial Garden
NAACP Headquarters

Ext. 6966

 4805 Mt. Hope Dr., Baltimore, MD 21215

MARYLAND BOOKSTORES

- ❑ A Likely Story Bookstore: Sykesville
- ❑ Atomic Books: Baltimore
- ❑ Baltimore Read Aloud: Baltimore
- ❑ Barston's Child's Play: Rockville
- ❑ Bird in Hand: Baltimore
- ❑ Bonjour Books DC: Kensington
- ❑ Books with a Past: Glenwood
- ❑ Books with a Past at Historic Savage Mill: Savage
- ❑ Caprichos Books: Bel Air
- ❑ Charm City Books: Baltimore
- ❑ Children's Book Garden: Ocean City
- ❑ Crackerjacks Toys and Children's Books: Easton
- ❑ Cricket Book Shop: Ashton
- ❑ Curious Iguana: Frederick
- ❑ Fenwick Street Used Books & Music: Leonardtown
- ❑ Greedy Reads: Baltimore
- ❑ Hullabaloo Book Company: California
- ❑ Lil' Books of Piety: Knoxville
- ❑ Loyalty Books: Silver Spring
- ❑ Main Street Books: Frostburg
- ❑ Mystery Loves Company: Oxford
- ❑ Novel Books: Clarksburg
- ❑ Old Fox Books & Coffeehouse: Annapolis
- ❑ Page After Page: Crownsville
- ❑ Paper Garden Used Books: Millersville
- ❑ Red Emma's Bookstore Coffeehouse: Baltimore
- ❑ Riches in Reading: Cheltenham
- ❑ Russia Online Bookstore: Kensington
- ❑ Sequitur Books: Boonsboro
- ❑ Station North Books: Baltimore
- ❑ The Annapolis Bookstore: Annapolis
- ❑ The Book Center: Cumberland
- ❑ The Children's Bookstore: Baltimore
- ❑ The Curmudgeon: Glen Burnie
- ❑ The Ivy Bookshop: Baltimore
- ❑ The Story House: Rockville
- ❑ Ukazoo Books: Towson
- ❑ White Rabbit Children's Books and Gifts: California

INTERVIEWS WITH MARYLAND BOOKSTORES

Ext. 9770

Listen to stories from some of our favorite bookshops in Maryland.

Edgar Allan Poe House & Museum

Ext. 4501

203 N. Amity St., Baltimore, MD 21223

 To hear any of these stories, dial 774-325-0503 and dial the four-digit extension.

Massachusetts

Little Women by Louisa May Alcott..........................1039
Little Women by Louisa May Alcott..........................5761
Prep by Curtis Sittenfeld..1050
The Bell Jar by Sylvia Plath....................................4465
The Bell Jar by Sylvia Plath....................................7577
The Handmaid's Tale by Margaret Atwood 6868
The Invention of Solitude by Paul Auster 2583
The Namesake by Jhumpa Lahiri.............................7886
The Scarlet Letter by Nathaniel Hawthorne............8909
The Storied Life of A. J. Fikry by Gabrielle Zevin 7914
Tuesdays with Morrie by Mitch Albom 6000

Salem Athenæum

Ext. 6275

 337 Essex St., Salem, MA 01970

INTERVIEWS WITH MASSACHUSETTS BOOKSTORES

Ext. 3769

Listen to stories from some of our favorite bookshops in Massachusetts.

Eric Carle Museum *of* Picture Book Art

Ext. 5201

 125 West Bay Rd., Amherst, MA 01002

Louisa May Alcott's Orchard House

Ext. 5878

399 Lexington Rd., Concord, MA 01742

MASSACHUSETTS BOOKSTORES

- ❑ A Great Yarn: Chatham
- ❑ Aesop's Fable: Holliston
- ❑ All She Wrote Books: Somerville
- ❑ Amherst Books: Amherst
- ❑ An Unlikely Story Plainville
- ❑ Andover Bookstore: Andover
- ❑ Barbara's Best Sellers: Boston
- ❑ Belmont Books: Belmont
- ❑ Book Ends: Winchester
- ❑ Book Moon: Easthampton
- ❑ Booklink Booksellers: Northampton
- ❑ Booklovers' Gourmet: Webster
- ❑ Books by the Sea: Centerville
- ❑ Boswell's Books: Shelburne Falls
- ❑ Broadside Bookshop: Northampton
- ❑ Brookline Booksmith: Brookline
- ❑ Bunch of Grapes Bookstore: Vineyard Haven
- ❑ Buttonwood Books and Toys: Cohasset
- ❑ Chapter Two Books: Williamstown
- ❑ Coffee Haven Books & Things: Holliston
- ❑ Copper Dog Books: Beverly
- ❑ East End Books Ptown: Provincetown
- ❑ Edgartown Books: Edgartown
- ❑ Eight Cousins: Falmouth
- ❑ El Taller Cafe and Bookstore: Lawrence
- ❑ Enchanted Passage: Sutton
- ❑ Frugal Bookstore: Roxbury
- ❑ Harvard Book Store: Cambridge
- ❑ High Five Books: Florence
- ❑ I AM Books: Boston
- ❑ Jabberwocky Bookshop: Newburyport
- ❑ Jenni Bick Bookbinding: Vineyard Haven
- ❑ Main Street Books: Orleans
- ❑ Mitchell's Book Corner: Nantucket
- ❑ Nantucket Bookworks: Nantucket
- ❑ Never Too Many Books: Peabody
- ❑ New England Mobile Book Fair: Newton Upper Falls
- ❑ Newtonville Books: Newton
- ❑ Odyssey Bookshop: South Hadley
- ❑ Pandemonium Books & Games: Cambridge
- ❑ Paperback Junction: South Easton
- ❑ Papercuts J.P.: Boston
- ❑ Park Street Books & Toys: Medfield
- ❑ Parnassus Book Service: Yarmouth Port
- ❑ Partners Village Store: Westport
- ❑ Porter Square Books: Cambridge
- ❑ Provincetown Bookshop: Provincetown
- ❑ Readmore Books: Taunton
- ❑ Root and Press Review: Worcester
- ❑ Roundabout Books: Greenfield
- ❑ Seven Stars: Cambridge
- ❑ Storybook Cove: Hanover
- ❑ Subtext Book Shop: New Bedford
- ❑ The Blue Bunny: Books and Toys: Dedham
- ❑ The Book Oasis: Stoneham
- ❑ The Book Rack: Arlington
- ❑ The Book Shop of Beverly Farms: Beverly

MASSACHUSETTS BOOKSTORES (CONT.)

- ❑ The Bookloft: Great Barrington
- ❑ The Bookstall: Marion
- ❑ The Bookstore: Lenox
- ❑ The Bookstore of Gloucester: Gloucester
- ❑ The Brewster Book Store: Brewster
- ❑ The Children's Book Shop: Brookline
- ❑ The Concord Bookshop: Concord
- ❑ The Montague Bookmill: Montague
- ❑ The Paper Store: Acton
- ❑ The Silver Unicorn Bookstore: Acton
- ❑ The Spirit of '76 Bookstore: Marblehead
- ❑ Titcomb's Bookshop: East Sandwich
- ❑ Trident Booksellers & Cafe: Boston
- ❑ Wellesley Books: Wellesley
- ❑ Westwinds Bookshop: Duxbury
- ❑ Where the Sidewalk Ends Bookstore: Chatham
- ❑ Whitelam Books: Reading
- ❑ Wicked Good Books: Salem
- ❑ World Eye Bookshop: Greenfield
- ❑ Yellow Umbrella Books: Chatham

Mental Health

Ariel by Sylvia Plath 4661
Cut by Patricia McCormick 7810
Frankenstein by Mary Shelley 1806
Furiously Happy by Jenny Lawson 8716
Inside the Walls of Troy by Clemence McLaren 7547
One Flew Over the Cuckoo's Nest by Ken Kesey 8633
The Bell Jar by Sylvia Plath 7577
The Bell Jar by Sylvia Plath 9832
The Collected Schizophrenias by Esmé Weijun Wang 9774
The Particular Sadness of Lemon Cake by Aimee Bender 7889
The Perks of Being a Wallflower by Stephen Chbosky 7580
The Tightrope Walker by Dorothy Gilman 7918

Michigan

Born on a Blue Day by Daniel Tammet 1981
Song of Solomon by Toni Morrison 9939

An important number:

Crisis Hotline

If you or someone you know is suicidal or in emotional distress, call this lifeline 24 hours a day, 7 days a week to speak with a trained crisis worker:

877-726-4727

MICHIGAN BOOKSTORES

- ❑ 2 Dandelions Bookshop: Brighton
- ❑ 27th Letter Books: Detroit
- ❑ A Bit of Earth: Flint
- ❑ Another Look Books: Taylor
- ❑ Archives Book Shop: East Lansing
- ❑ Argos Book Shop: Grand Rapids
- ❑ Baker Book House: Grand Rapids
- ❑ Bay Books: Suttons Bay
- ❑ Bestsellers Bookstore & Coffee: Mason
- ❑ Between the Covers: Harbor Springs
- ❑ Black Stone Bookstore: Ypsilanti
- ❑ Book Beat: Oak Park
- ❑ Book Nook: Monroe
- ❑ Book Suey: Hamtramck
- ❑ Bookbound: Ann Arbor
- ❑ Bookbrokers & Kramer's Cafe: Traverse City
- ❑ Bookbug: Kalamazoo
- ❑ Books & Mortar: Grand Rapids
- ❑ Books Connection: Livonia
- ❑ Boston Tea Room: Ferndale
- ❑ Brilliant Books: Traverse City
- ❑ Buy the Book: Kawkawlin
- ❑ Canterbury Book Store: Escanaba
- ❑ Carol's Paperbacks Plus: Waterford
- ❑ Common Language Bookstore: Ann Arbor
- ❑ Cottage Book Shop: Glen Arbor
- ❑ Crazy Wisdom Bookstore & Tearoom: Ann Arbor
- ❑ Curious Book Shop: East Lansing
- ❑ Detroit Book City Bookstore: Southfield
- ❑ Epilogue Books: Rockford
- ❑ Everybody Reads: Books & Stuff: Lansing
- ❑ Fenton's Open Book: Fenton
- ❑ Forever Books: St. Joseph
- ❑ Grandpa's Barn: Copper Harbor
- ❑ Hope Geneva Bookstore: Holland
- ❑ Horizon Books: Cadillac, Traverse City
- ❑ Island Books & Crafts: Sault Ste. Marie
- ❑ Island Bookstore: Mackinac Island
- ❑ Kazoo Books: Kalamazoo
- ❑ Lakeside Books: Benton Harbor
- ❑ Leelanau Books: Leland
- ❑ Leopard Print Books: Saginaw
- ❑ Literati Bookstore: Ann Arbor
- ❑ Louhelen Bahá'i School Bookstore: Davison
- ❑ Lowry's Books and More: Sturgis, Three Rivers
- ❑ McLean & Eakin Booksellers: Petoskey
- ❑ Michigan News Agency: Kalamazoo
- ❑ Nicola's Books: Ann Arbor
- ❑ Owosso Books & Beans: Owosso
- ❑ Pages Bookshop: Detroit
- ❑ Purple Tree Books: Cheboygan
- ❑ R&B Used Books: Grand Blanc
- ❑ Reader's World: Holland
- ❑ Round Lake Bookstore: Charlevoix
- ❑ Saturn Booksellers: Gaylord
- ❑ Schuler Books: Grand Rapids, Okemos
- ❑ Serendipity Books: Chelsea
- ❑ Singapore Bank Bookstore: Saugatuck
- ❑ Snowbound Books: Marquette
- ❑ Source Booksellers: Detroit
- ❑ Squirreled Away Books: Armada
- ❑ Stirling Books & Brew: Albion
- ❑ The Bluestocking Bookshop: Holland
- ❑ The Book Nook & Java Shop: Montague

MICHIGAN BOOKSTORES

- ❑ The Bookman: Grand Haven
- ❑ The Booknook: East Tawas
- ❑ The Bookstore: Frankfort
- ❑ The Mitten Word Bookshop: Marshall
- ❑ Third Mind Books: Ann Arbor
- ❑ This Is a Bookstore: Kalamazoo
- ❑ Totem Books: Flint
- ❑ Turn the Page: Alpena
- ❑ UGRR Reading Station Bookstore: Detroit
- ❑ We are LIT: Grand Rapids

INTERVIEWS WITH MICHIGAN BOOKSTORES

Ext. 9771

Listen to stories from some of our favorite bookshops in Michigan.

Fox River Pathway

Ext. 6276

Seney Township, MI 49883

Minnesota

Sidewalk Poetry

Ext. 5879

St. Paul, MN

MINNESOTA BOOKSTORES

- ❑ Babycake's Book Stack: St. Paul
- ❑ Beagle and Wolf Books & Bindery: Park Rapids
- ❑ Bexter Book & Copy: Milaca
- ❑ Birchbark Books and Gifts: Grand Marais
- ❑ Birchbark Books and Native Arts: Minneapolis
- ❑ Boneshaker Books: Minneapolis
- ❑ Buffalo Books & Coffee: Buffalo
- ❑ Cherry Street Books: Alexandria
- ❑ Collective Books & Records: Rochester
- ❑ Content Bookstore: Northfield
- ❑ Cream & Amber: Hopkins
- ❑ Daybreak Press Global Bookshop: Minneapolis
- ❑ Drury Lane Books: Grand Marais
- ❑ Excelsior Bay Books: Excelsior
- ❑ Eye of Horus Metaphysical: Minneapolis
- ❑ Fair Trade Books: Red Wing
- ❑ Half Price Books: Apple Valley, Coon Rapids, Crystal, Maplewood, Roseville, St. Louis Park, St. Paul
- ❑ Kiddywampus: Hopkins
- ❑ Lake Country Booksellers: White Bear Lake
- ❑ Little Professor Book Center: Owatonna
- ❑ Magers & Quinn Booksellers: Minneapolis
- ❑ Milkweed Books: Minneapolis
- ❑ Moon Palace Books: Minneapolis
- ❑ Next Chapter Booksellers: St. Paul
- ❑ Oleanna Books: Minneapolis
- ❑ Once Upon a Crime: Minneapolis
- ❑ Otter Lane Book Shop: Anoka
- ❑ Paperback Exchange: Minneapolis
- ❑ Paperbacks and Pieces: Winona
- ❑ Piragis Northwoods Company: Ely
- ❑ Red Balloon Bookshop: St. Paul
- ❑ Scout & Morgan Books: Cambridge
- ❑ Silver Lake Books: Rochester
- ❑ Storied Owl Books: St. Paul
- ❑ Subtext Books: St. Paul
- ❑ Sweet Peas & Back Forty Books: Two Harbors
- ❑ Sweet Reads: Austin
- ❑ The Bookstore at Fitger's: Duluth
- ❑ The Irreverent Bookworm: Minneapolis
- ❑ The Village Bookstore: Grand Rapids
- ❑ The Willow Bookstore: Perham
- ❑ Turtle Town Books & Gifts: Nisswa
- ❑ Valley Bookseller: Stillwater
- ❑ Victor Lundeen Company: Fergus Falls
- ❑ Wild Rumpus: Minneapolis
- ❑ Zenith Bookstore: Duluth

INTERVIEWS WITH MINNESOTA BOOKSTORES

Ext. 2349

Listen to stories from some of our favorite bookshops in Minnesota.

Misfits

Alice's Adventures in Wonderland by Lewis Carroll....3652
Anthem by Ayn Rand....9326
Divergent by Veronica Roth....7579
I Am Not Myself These Days by Josh Kilmer-Purcell....5986
I'm with the Band by Pamela Des Barres....7739
Just Kids by Patti Smith....9841
My Name Is Asher Lev by Chaim Potok....4609
Stargirl by Jerry Spinelli....1009
The Hitchhiker's Guide to the Galaxy by Douglas Adams....4242
The Perks of Being a Wallflower by Stephen Chbosky....7808
The Phantom Tollbooth by Norton Juster....9099

Mississippi

32 Candles by Ernessa T. Carter....7553
Sing, Unburied, Sing by Jesmyn Ward....3941

INTERVIEWS WITH MISSISSIPPI BOOKSTORES

Ext. 9779

Listen to stories from some of our favorite bookshops in Mississippi.

MISSISSIPPI BOOKSTORES

- ❑ Bay Books: Bay St. Louis
- ❑ Book Mart & Cafe: Starkville
- ❑ Lemuria Books: Jackson
- ❑ Lorelei Books: Vicksburg
- ❑ Main Street Books: Hattiesburg
- ❑ Off Square Books: Oxford
- ❑ Pass Christian Books: Pass Christian
- ❑ Rare Square Books: Oxford
- ❑ Reed's Gum Tree Bookstore: Tupelo
- ❑ SAGE Coffee & Books: Starkville
- ❑ Southern Bound Book Shop: Biloxi
- ❑ Square Books: Oxford
- ❑ Square Books Jr.: Oxford
- ❑ Turnrow Book Co.: Greenwood
- ❑ Violet Valley Bookstore: Water Valley

William Faulkner's Grave at Saint Peter's Cemetery

Ext. 3996

Corner of Jefferson Ave. and N. 16th St., Oxford, MS 38655

Margaret Walker Center

Ext. 5202

Ayer Hall
Jackson State University
Jackson, MS 39203

Eudora Welty House and Garden

Ext. 4687

1109 Pinehurst St., Jackson, MS 39202

Missouri

Laura Ingalls Wilder Historic Home & Museum

Ext. 3997

3060 Highway A
Mansfield, MO 65704

Kansas City Public Library

Ext. 5436

14 W. 10th St.
Kansas City, MO 64105

INTERVIEWS WITH MISSOURI BOOKSTORES

Ext. 7251

Listen to stories from some of our favorite bookshops in Missouri.

MISSOURI BOOKSTORES

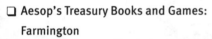

- ❑ Aesop's Treasury Books and Games: Farmington
- ❑ Cavener's Library and Office Supplies: Nevada
- ❑ Country Sunshine: Republic
- ❑ Downtown Book & Toy: Jefferson City
- ❑ Dunaway Books: St. Louis
- ❑ EyeSeeMe African American Children's Bookstore: University City
- ❑ Half Price Books: Chesterfield, Independence, Kansas City, St. Louis
- ❑ Left Bank Books: St. Louis
- ❑ Main Street Books: St. Charles
- ❑ Meet Me St. Louis: St. Louis
- ❑ Missouri State Bookstore: Springfield
- ❑ Neighborhood Reads: Washington
- ❑ Our Daily Nada: Kansas City
- ❑ Pagination Bookshop: Springfield
- ❑ Reader's World: Sedalia
- ❑ River Reader Books: Lexington
- ❑ Rose's Bookhouse: O'Fallon
- ❑ Skylark Bookshop: Columbia
- ❑ Stonecrest Book & Toy: Osage Beach
- ❑ Subterranean Books: St. Louis
- ❑ The Book House: St. Louis
- ❑ The Book Rack: Cape Girardeau
- ❑ The Novel Neighbor: Webster Groves
- ❑ The Owl Books & Brew: Kansas City
- ❑ The Red Hen Bookshop: Hannibal
- ❑ Uriel's Unusual Bookstore: Springfield
- ❑ Village Books: Columbia
- ❑ Well Read: Fulton
- ❑ Yellow Dog Bookshop: Columbia

Mistakes

Monsters

Montana

INTERVIEWS WITH MONTANA BOOKSTORES

Ext. 1353

Listen to stories from some of our favorite bookshops in Montana.

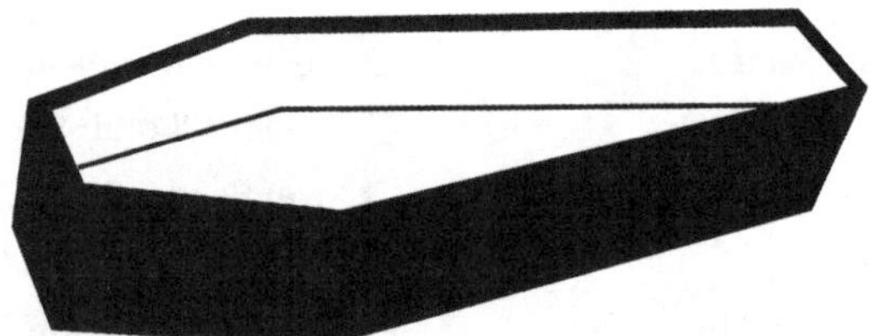

VAMPIRE SUPPLY CO.

Everything you need for your favorite undead!

Blood bottles (in all types!)
Blackout shades (in two colors: noir and midnight!)
Coffin decor, and more!

Call: 1036

 To hear any of these stories, dial 774-325-0503 and dial the four-digit extension.

MONTANA BOOKSTORES

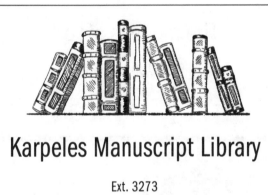

- ❑ Barjon's Books: Billings
- ❑ Bookworks of Whitefish: Whitefish
- ❑ Browsing Bison Books: Deer Lodge
- ❑ Chapter One Book Store: Hamilton
- ❑ Country Bookshelf: Bozeman
- ❑ Elk River Books: Livingston
- ❑ Fact & Fiction: Missoula
- ❑ Montana Book Company: Helena
- ❑ Montana Farmacy: Eureka
- ❑ Montana Valley Book Store: Alberton
- ❑ Reading Leaves: Townsend
- ❑ The Book Exchange: Missoula
- ❑ The Bookstore: Dillon
- ❑ This House of Books: Billings

Karpeles Manuscript Library

Ext. 3273

 1300 1st Ave., N. Great Falls, MT 59401

Mothers

Blessings by Anna Quindlen 7816
Dandelion Wine by Ray Bradbury 4601
Flip, Flap, Fly!: A Book for Babies Everywhere
by Phyllis Root 7338
Good Dog, Carl by Alexandra Day 8723
Harry Potter series by J. K. Rowling 6342
Lace by Shirley Conran 7666
Making Toast by Roger Rosenblatt 5768
Not in God's Name by Jonathan Sacks 3784
"Of the Terrible Doubt of Appearances" by
Walt Whitman 3792
Stranger in a Strange Land by Robert A. Heinlein 1828
The Darkest Child by Delores Phillips 4847
The End of Your Life Book Club by Will Schwalbe 1123

An anonymous voicemail message about

Lace

by Shirley Conran

Ext. 7666

"Which one of you bitches is my mother?" That's the line that hooked me with this book. I was adopted at birth and I wanted desperately to find my birth mother, mostly out of curiosity but also because at the time I was trying to get pregnant with my first child and the doctor was asking me all kinds of questions about my medical history and I couldn't answer any of them. It was a really long search. It took a couple of years and there were lots of twists and turns, but in the end I prevailed and I found her. We spent probably six or eight months writing each other letters. We talked once on the phone and eventually we made plans to meet in person. Sadly, she passed away before that happened. It was rather sudden, but in retrospect just finding her gave me a sense of peace and closure, and most of all it made me really appreciate my real mom—the amazing woman who raised me—even more. ☎

The Little Prince by Antoine de Saint-Exupéry.........3223
The Namesake by Jhumpa Lahiri............................7886
The Neverending Story by Michael Ende.................7568
The Night Circus by Erin Morgenstern.....................4606
Wave by Sonali Deraniyagala................................2944

Moving

A Wrinkle in Time by Madeleine L'Engle..................2359
Breakfast at Tiffany's by Truman Capote.................4607
Dandelion Wine by Ray Bradbury...........................7571
Escape from Asylum by Madeleine Roux.................1982
The Complete Sherlock Holmes by Sir Arthur Conan Doyle...4603
The Fan Man by William Kotzwinkle........................7556
The Fault in Our Stars by John Green.......................6751
The Glass Menagerie by Tennessee Williams..........6859
The Sibley Guide to Birds by David Allen Sibley......9908

Music

Born to Run by Bruce Springsteen..........................5672
Girl by Blake Nelson...8721
Harry Potter series by J. K. Rowling.........................1371
I'm with the Band by Pamela Des Barres.................7739
The Catcher in the Rye by J. D. Salinger..................2841

2 Guys Moving Co.

The move is afoot!

Call John: 4603

YOU'VE GOT IT

Guitar Lessons For You

Learn music with a Human Touch . . .

Call Rosalita to schedule: 5672

The Great Gatsby by F. Scott Fitzgerald 6345
The Mozart Season by Virginia Euwer Wolff 7884

Nature

48 Peaks: Hiking and Healing in the White Mountains by Cheryl Suchors 8638
A River Runs Through It by Norman Maclean 3648
A Short History of Nearly Everything by Bill Bryson 7722
Dear America: Voyage on the Titanic by Ellen Emerson White 6684
Fundamental Formulas of Physics edited by Donald H. Menzel 7555
Great Plains by Michael Forsberg............................8636
Into the Wild by Jon Krakauer..................................7744
Jurassic Park by Michael Crichton 2001
Pilgrim at Tinker Creek by Annie Dillard 4605
The Lord of the Rings by J. R. R. Tolkien...................7811

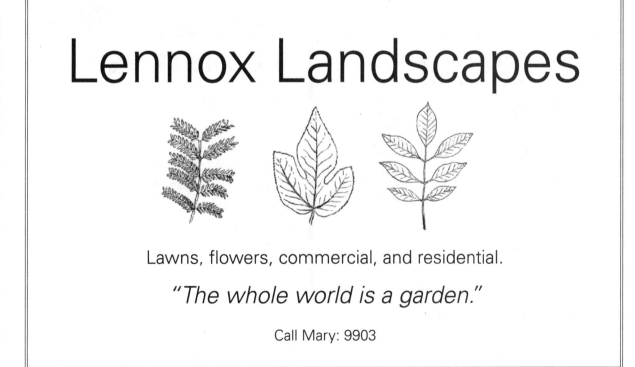

An anonymous voicemail message about

Pilgrim at Tinker Creek by Annie Dillard

Ext. 4605

Annie Dillard's *Pilgrim at Tinker Creek* was published in 1974, which was the year I was born. It's a book that's influenced the way I see the natural world. The book legitimizes taking a walk, taking a saunter, sitting down by the creek. The message is *Something's gonna happen. You'll find something. You'll see something.* And it's profoundly affected the way I live, the way that I value the place that I live. No matter what your jam is, if you're into finding mushrooms or you're into watching birds or you climb mountains or you run rivers or you hunt, you fish. Annie Dillard's message is *Do it. Get out there. Even if it's a hundred degrees outside. Even if it's the middle of winter and everything seems kind of frozen. Like, get out, get wet, get your lips chapped.* And that's my book. *Pilgrim at Tinker Creek.* It's a keeper. ☎

The Martian by Andy Weir....................1051
The Oldest Living Things in the World by Rachel Sussman....................7563
The Secret Garden by Frances Hodgson Burnett....................7843
The Secret Garden by Frances Hodgson Burnett....................9903
Thirst by Mary Oliver....................1003
Where the Crawdads Sing by Delia Owens....................2945

Nebraska

Fangirl by Rainbow Rowell....................9708
Great Plains by Michael Forsberg....................8636
My Ántonia by Willa Cather....................9823

INTERVIEWS WITH NEBRASKA BOOKSTORES

Ext. 3367

Listen to stories from some of our favorite bookshops in Nebraska.

NEBRASKA BOOKSTORES

- ❑ A Novel Idea Bookstore: Lincoln
- ❑ Badger's Bookshop: Lincoln
- ❑ Chapters Books & Gifts: Seward
- ❑ Dundee Book Company: Omaha
- ❑ Francie and Finch Bookshop: Lincoln
- ❑ Gloria Deo: Lincoln, Omaha
- ❑ Half Price Books: Omaha
- ❑ Indigo Bridge Books & Cafe: Lincoln
- ❑ Plains Trading Company: Valentine
- ❑ The Bookworm: Omaha
- ❑ The Next Chapter: Omaha
- ❑ The Re-Find Reader: North Platte
- ❑ The Sequel Bookshop: Kearney

Willa Cather House and Memorial Prairie

Ext. 6455

425 N. Webster St. #2466
Red Cloud, NE 68970

Nerds

Nevada

An anonymous voicemail message about

The Elements by Theodore Gray

Ext. 7203

I just wanted to mention the book *The Elements* by Theodore Gray. It's a book that celebrates the periodic table through these beautiful, full-page, gorgeous images. When I read this I was just a little nerdy kid in sixth grade with next to no friends. But this book showed me that you can really love something, even if it's something like science. You can love something fully and kind of unequivocally just because it's so amazing and awesome. That's kind of how I've defined the word "nerd" ever since. I've identified as a nerd because to me that just means loving something totally. I've found all sorts of stuff that I love, and once you start loving something, you can kind of start loving yourself, and I guess you can start talking to other people about stuff that they love unequivocally, and it ends up that you make a lot of friends through this process. And last year I was elected class president. So yeah. That's it. ☎

Clark County Museum Collection of Vegas Fiction

1830 S. Boulder Hwy., Henderson, NV 89002

Ext. 2204

NEVADA BOOKSTORES

- ❑ Grassroots Books: Reno
- ❑ Sundance Books and Music: Reno
- ❑ The Writer's Block: Las Vegas

Circus Circus Casino

Ext. 6456

2880 S. Las Vegas Blvd.
Las Vegas, NV 89109

INTERVIEWS WITH NEVADA BOOKSTORES

Ext. 2350

Listen to stories from some of our favorite bookshops in Nevada.

New Hampshire

48 Peaks: Hiking and Healing in the White Mountains by Cheryl Suchors 8638
Wintergirls by Laurie Halse Anderson 7814

Robert Frost Farm

Ext. 2621

122 Rockingham Rd.
Derry, NH 03038

INTERVIEWS WITH NEW HAMPSHIRE BOOKSTORES

Ext. 1352

Listen to stories from some of our favorite bookshops in New Hampshire.

NEW HAMPSHIRE BOOKSTORES

- ❑ A Freethinker's Corner: Dover
- ❑ Alran Books: Harrisville
- ❑ Annie's Book Stop: Laconia
- ❑ Bayswater Book Co.: Center Harbor
- ❑ Bookery Manchester: Manchester
- ❑ Bull Moose: Keene, Portsmouth, Salem
- ❑ G. Willikers! Books & Toys: Portsmouth
- ❑ Gibson's Bookstore: Concord
- ❑ Innisfree Bookshop: Meredith
- ❑ Little Village Toy & Book Shop: Littleton
- ❑ MainStreet BookEnds of Warner: Warner
- ❑ Morgan Hill Bookstore: New London
- ❑ RiverRun Bookstore: Portsmouth
- ❑ Sheafe Street Books: Portsmouth
- ❑ The Country Bookseller: Wolfeboro
- ❑ The Toadstool Bookshop: Keene, Nashua, Peterborough
- ❑ Treehouse Toys: Portsmouth
- ❑ Water Street Bookstore: Exeter
- ❑ White Birch Books: North Conway
- ❑ YJ's Boxes of Books: Nashua

POLYANNA STATUE

Ext. 5437

92 Main St.
Littleton, NH 03561

Allen Ginsberg's Grave at Gomel Chesed Cemetery

Ext. 3263

245 Mt. Olivet Ave., Newark, NJ 07114

INTERVIEWS WITH NEW JERSEY BOOKSTORES

Ext. 1354

Listen to stories from some of our favorite bookshops in New Jersey.

New Jersey

13 Little Blue Envelopes by Maureen Johnson 3355
Americanah by Chimamanda Ngozi Adichie 4658
Born to Run by Bruce Springsteen 5672
Boy Meets Boy by David Levithan 3427
Tiger Eyes by Judy Blume 3046

New Mexico

Brave New World by Aldous Huxley.........................5673
Their Eyes Were Watching God by Zora Neale Hurston 5927
Tiger Eyes by Judy Blume 3046

NEW JERSEY BOOKSTORES

- ❑ Alomo Books: South Orange
- ❑ ANT Bookstore & Cafe: Clifton
- ❑ Black Dog Books: Lafayette
- ❑ Bookends: Ridgewood
- ❑ Books & Greetings: Northvale
- ❑ Books, Bytes & Beyond: Fair Lawn
- ❑ BookTowne: Manasquan
- ❑ Booktrader of Hamilton: Hamilton
- ❑ Califon Bookshop: Califon
- ❑ Eleventh Step Books: Haddon Township
- ❑ Fieldstone Book Company: Wyckoff
- ❑ Footnotes Bookstore: Clifton
- ❑ Inkwood Books: Haddonfield
- ❑ jaZams: Princeton
- ❑ Kinokuniya: Edgewater
- ❑ Labyrinth Books: Princeton
- ❑ Little City Books: Hoboken
- ❑ Montclair Book Center: Montclair
- ❑ Re-Turn the Page: Williamstown
- ❑ Respectrum Books: Sussex
- ❑ River Road Books: Fair Haven
- ❑ Short Stories Bookshop & Community Hub: Madison
- ❑ Sparkhouse: South Orange
- ❑ Sparta Books: Sparta
- ❑ Sun Rose Words & Music: Ocean City
- ❑ The Bear and the Books: Hopewell
- ❑ The Book Garden: Frenchtown
- ❑ The Bookworm: Bernardsville
- ❑ The Bookworm: Surf City
- ❑ The Curious Reader: Glen Rock
- ❑ The Little Boho Bookshop: Bayonne
- ❑ The Paper Peddler: Cape May Court House
- ❑ The Town Book Store: Westfield
- ❑ Watchung Booksellers: Montclair
- ❑ WORD: Jersey City
- ❑ Words!: Asbury Park
- ❑ Words Bookstore: Livingston, Maplewood

NEW MEXICO BOOKSTORES

- ❏ Amy's Bookcase: Farmington
- ❏ Barbara's Bookstore: Santa Fe
- ❏ Bee Hive: Santa Fe
- ❏ Books Etcetera: Ruidoso
- ❏ Bookworks: Albuquerque
- ❏ Bowlin's Mesilla Book Center: Mesilla
- ❏ Casa Camino Real Book Store & Art Gallery: Las Cruces
- ❏ Collected Works Bookstore & Coffeehouse: Santa Fe
- ❏ Duende District Bookstore at Red Planet: Albuquerque
- ❏ Garcia Street Books: Santa Fe
- ❏ Op.cit.: Santa Fe
- ❏ Organic Books: Albuquerque
- ❏ Page 1 Books: Albuquerque
- ❏ Quirky Books: Albuquerque
- ❏ Title Wave Books: Albuquerque
- ❏ Tome on the Range: Las Vegas
- ❏ Turn the Page Books and More: Clovis
- ❏ Your Book Obsession: Albuquerque

George R. R. Martin's Jean Cocteau Cinema

Ext. 5679

418 Montezuma Ave., Santa Fe, NM 87501

D. H. Lawrence Ranch

Ext. 2622

Lawrence Ranch Rd.
Arroyo Seco, NM 87514

INTERVIEWS WITH NEW MEXICO BOOKSTORES

Ext. 6933

Listen to stories from some of our favorite bookshops in New Mexico.

INTERVIEWS WITH NEW YORK BOOKSTORES

Ext. 3368

Listen to stories from some of our favorite bookshops in New York.

New York

Cat's Cradle by Kurt Vonnegut 5677
The Great Gatsby by F. Scott Fitzgerald 6866
The Great Gatsby by F. Scott Fitzgerald 6867

Sleepy Hollow

Ext. 8134 Sleepy Hollow, NY

Mark Twain Room

at the Buffalo & Erie County Public Library

1 Lafayette Square, Buffalo, NY 14203

Ext. 3264

NEW YORK BOOKSTORES

- ❑ A to Z Books: Orchard Park
- ❑ Adirondack Reader: Inlet
- ❑ Albion Books: Buffalo
- ❑ Andersons Larchmont: Larchmont
- ❑ Anime Castle: Flushing
- ❑ Arcade Booksellers: Rye
- ❑ Battenkill Books: Cambridge
- ❑ Berry and Co.: Sag Harbor
- ❑ Binnacle Books: Beacon
- ❑ Blue Door Books: Cedarhurst
- ❑ Book House of Stuyvesant Plaza: Albany
- ❑ Book Revue: Huntington
- ❑ Bookburgh Books: Plattsburgh
- ❑ BookHampton: East Hampton
- ❑ Booksy Galore: Pound Ridge
- ❑ Briars & Brambles Books: Windham
- ❑ Bronx River Books: Scarsdale
- ❑ Buffalo Street Books: Ithaca
- ❑ Burning Books: Buffalo
- ❑ Canio's Books: Sag Harbor
- ❑ Card Carrying Books & Gifts: Corning
- ❑ Chautauqua Bookstore: Chautauqua
- ❑ Creative Corner Books: Hobart
- ❑ Cuppa Pulp Writers' Space: Chestnut Ridge
- ❑ Dog Ears Bookstore: Buffalo
- ❑ Element of Fun: Rochester
- ❑ Finley's Fiction: Shelter Island Heights
- ❑ Flights of Fantasy Books & Games: Albany
- ❑ Galapagos Books: Hastings-on-Hudson
- ❑ Green Toad Bookstore: Oneonta
- ❑ Half Moon Books: Kingston
- ❑ Hipocampo Children's Books: Rochester
- ❑ Hobart Book Village: Hobart
- ❑ Hobart International Bookport: Hobart
- ❑ I Love Books: Delmar
- ❑ Inquiring Minds Bookstore: New Paltz, Saugerties
- ❑ Kayleighbug Books: Morristown
- ❑ Kew and Willow Books: Kew Gardens
- ❑ Lake City Books and Writers' Nook: Plattsburgh
- ❑ Lift Bridge Book Shop: Brockport
- ❑ Little Joe's: Katonah
- ❑ Locust Valley Bookstore: Locust Valley
- ❑ Main Street Beat: Nyack
- ❑ Main Street Book Company: White Plains
- ❑ Market Block Books: Troy
- ❑ Meadowlark Toys and Sunbridge Books: Spring Valley
- ❑ Merritt Bookstore: Millbrook
- ❑ Monkey See, Monkey Do . . . Children's Bookstore: Clarence
- ❑ Mysteries on Main Street: Johnstown
- ❑ Northshire Bookstore: Saratoga Springs
- ❑ Oblong Books & Music: Millerton, Rhinebeck
- ❑ Off the Beaten Path Bookstore: Lakewood
- ❑ One Grand Books: Narrowsburg
- ❑ Pickwick Book Shop: Nyack
- ❑ Postmark Books: Rosendale
- ❑ Rough Draft Bar & Books: Kingston
- ❑ Sag Harbor Books: Sag Harbor
- ❑ Scattered Books: Chappaqua
- ❑ Southampton Books: Southampton
- ❑ Split Rock Books: Cold Spring

NEW YORK BOOKSTORES (CONT.)

- ❑ Talking Leaves . . . Books: Buffalo
- ❑ The Barking Goose: Newburgh
- ❑ The Biblio-Tech Café: Perry
- ❑ The Book Corner: Niagra Falls
- ❑ The Book Cove: Pawling
- ❑ The Book Nook: Saranac Lake
- ❑ The Bookstore Plus Music & Art: Lake Placid
- ❑ The Chatham Bookstore: Chatham
- ❑ The Dog Eared Book: Palmyra
- ❑ The Dolphin Bookshop: Port Washington
- ❑ The Golden Notebook: Woodstock
- ❑ The Open Door Bookstore: Schenectady
- ❑ The River's End Bookstore: Oswego
- ❑ The Scholar's Choice: Rochester
- ❑ The Spotty Dog Books & Ale: Hudson
- ❑ The Three Arts Bookstore: Poughkeepsie
- ❑ The Treehouse Reading & Arts Center: New York Mills
- ❑ The Village Bookstore: Pleasantville
- ❑ The Voracious Reader: New Rochelle
- ❑ Toy Loft: East Aurora
- ❑ Westside Stories Used Books: Buffalo
- ❑ White Paw Books & Curiosities: Newark
- ❑ Womrath Bookshop: Bronxville

New York City

A Little Life by Hanya Yanagihara............................2643
A Tree Grows in Brooklyn by Betty Smith 1020
A Tree Grows in Brooklyn by Betty Smith 8629
American Psycho by Bret Easton Ellis 4657

James Baldwin House

Ext. 9839

137 W. 71st St., New York, NY 10023

White Horse Tavern

Ext. 5680

567 Hudson St.
New York, NY 10014

 To hear any of these stories, dial 774-325-0503 and dial the four-digit extension.

Langston Hughes House

Ext. 9827

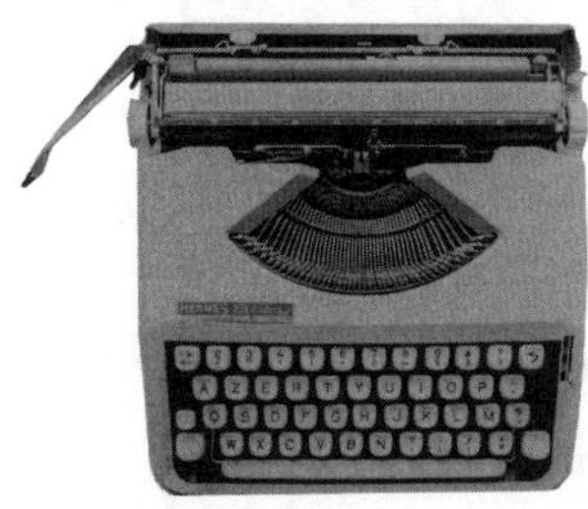

20 E. 127th St. New York, NY 10035

INTERVIEWS WITH NEW YORK CITY BOOKSTORES

Ext. 6935

Listen to stories from some of our favorite bookshops in New York City.

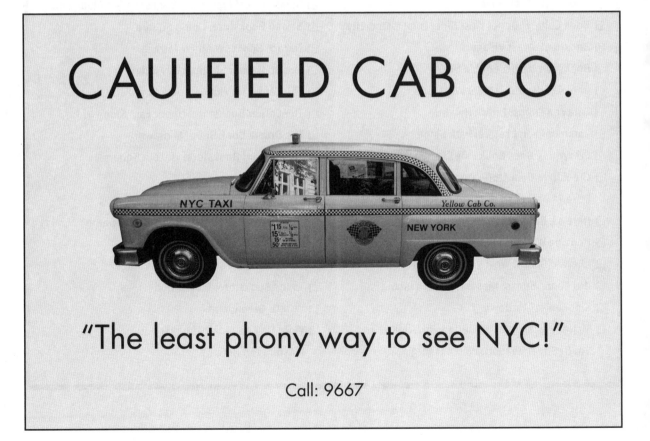

CAULFIELD CAB CO.

"The least phony way to see NYC!"

Call: 9667

NEW YORK CITY BOOKSTORES

- ❑ 192 Books: Chelsea
- ❑ Archestratus Books & Foods: Greenpoint
- ❑ Astoria Bookshop: Astoria
- ❑ Avoid the Day Bookstore & Cafe: Rockaway Beach
- ❑ Bank Street Bookstore: Upper West Side
- ❑ Bluestockings: Lower East Side
- ❑ Boogie Down Books: Bronx
- ❑ Book Club: East Village
- ❑ Book Culture: Upper West Side, Long Island City
- ❑ Bookbook: West Village
- ❑ Books Are Magic: Cobble Hill
- ❑ Books of Wonder: Upper West Side
- ❑ Cafe con Libros: Crown Heights
- ❑ Community Bookstore: Park Slope
- ❑ Everything Goes Book Cafe: Staten Island
- ❑ Greenlight Bookstore: Fort Greene, Prospect Lefferts Gardens
- ❑ Here's a Book Store: Sheepshead Bay
- ❑ Housing Works Bookstore Cafe & Bar: Soho
- ❑ Idlewild Books: West Village, Cobble Hill
- ❑ JHU Comic Books: Kips Bay, Staten Island
- ❑ Kinokuniya: Midtown
- ❑ McNally Jackson Books: Citypoint, Nolita, South Street Seaport, Williamsburg
- ❑ Mil Mundos Books: Bushwick
- ❑ Posman Books: Chelsea Market, Rockefeller Center
- ❑ PowerHouse on 8th: Park Slope
- ❑ Revolution Books: Harlem
- ❑ Rizzoli Bookstore: NoMad
- ❑ Shakespeare & Co.: Upper East Side, Upper West Side
- ❑ Sisters Uptown Bookstore: Harlem
- ❑ Spoonbill & Sugartown, Booksellers: Williamsburg
- ❑ Strand Bookstore: Union Square
- ❑ Terrace Books: Windsor Terrace
- ❑ The BookMark Shoppe: Bay Ridge
- ❑ The Center for Fiction Bookstore: Fort Greene
- ❑ The Corner Bookstore: Upper East Side
- ❑ The Drama Book Shop: Midtown
- ❑ The Juilliard Bookstore: Lincoln Square
- ❑ The Lit. Bar: Bronx
- ❑ The Mysterious Bookshop: Tribeca
- ❑ The PowerHouse Arena Bookstore: Dumbo
- ❑ The Schomburg Shop: Harlem
- ❑ Three Lives & Company: West Village
- ❑ Topos Bookstore: Ridgewood
- ❑ WORD: Greenpoint
- ❑ Word Up Community Bookshop: Washington Heights

 To hear any of these stories, dial 774-325-0503 and dial the four-digit extension.

Angela's Ashes by Frank McCourt 7842
Boom by Michael Shnayerson 5671
Breakfast at Tiffany's by Truman Capote 4607
Extremely Loud and Incredibly Close by
Jonathan Safran Foer 8703
From the Mixed-Up Files of Mrs. Basil E.
Frankweiler by E. L. Konigsburg 1024
Invisible Man by Ralph Ellison 1235
Just Kids by Patti Smith 9841
Let the Great World Spin by
Colum McCann...9501
Red at the Bone by Jacqueline Woodson 1833
Rosemary's Baby by
Ira Levin...1808
Severance by Ling Ma...1811
Sweetbitter by Stephanie Danler 1827
The Catcher in the Rye by J. D. Salinger...................7809
The Catcher in the Rye by J. D. Salinger...................9667

North Carolina

The Curious Charms of Arthur Pepper by
Phaedra Patrick 3845
The Notebook by Nicholas Sparks............................7887

NORTH CAROLINA BOOKSTORES

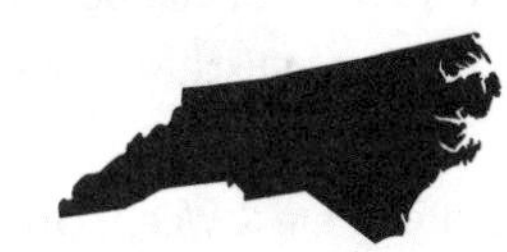

- ❑ Adventure Bound Books: Morganton
- ❑ Angel Wings Bookstore: Stem
- ❑ Battery Park Book Exchange: Asheville
- ❑ Blue Ridge Books: Waynesville
- ❑ Bookmarks: Winston-Salem
- ❑ Books to Be Red: Ocracoke
- ❑ Books Unlimited: Franklin
- ❑ Boomerang Bookshop: Greensboro
- ❑ Brooks Preik: Wilmington
- ❑ Buxton Village Books: Buxton
- ❑ Calico Paw Books & Gifts: Henderson
- ❑ Chapter 2: Cashiers
- ❑ Chelsea Antiques: Durham
- ❑ City Lights Bookstore: Sylva
- ❑ Coastal Cottage Life: Belhaven
- ❑ Cultivator: Murfreesboro
- ❑ Dee Gee's Gifts & Books: Morehead City
- ❑ Downtown Book & News: Asheville
- ❑ Downtown Books: Manteo
- ❑ Duck's Cottage: Duck
- ❑ Edward McKay Used Books & More: Greensboro, Winston-Salem
- ❑ Emerald Isle Books and Toys: Emerald Isle
- ❑ Epilogue Books Chocolate Brews: Chapel Hill
- ❑ Episcopal Shoppe: Fayetteville
- ❑ Firestorm Books & Coffee: Asheville
- ❑ Flyleaf Books: Chapel Hill
- ❑ Foggy Pine Books: Boone
- ❑ Given Book Shop: Pinehurst
- ❑ Golden Fig Books: Durham
- ❑ Gone Fishing Books: Lenoir
- ❑ Highland Books: Brevard
- ❑ John Neal Bookseller: Greensboro
- ❑ Letters Bookshop: Durham
- ❑ Liberation's Station: Raleigh
- ❑ Little Switzerland Books & Beans: Little Switzerland
- ❑ Main Street Books: Davidson
- ❑ Malaprop's Bookstore/Cafe: Asheville

NORTH CAROLINA BOOKSTORES (CONT.)

- ❑ McIntyre's Books: Pittsboro
- ❑ Millie's Used Books: Franklin
- ❑ Mr. K's Used Books, Music and More: Asheville
- ❑ Page 158 Books: Wake Forest
- ❑ Page After Page Bookstore: Elizabeth City
- ❑ Park Road Books: Charlotte
- ❑ Pomegranate Books: Wilmington
- ❑ Purple Crow Books: Hillsborough
- ❑ Quail Ridge Books: Raleigh
- ❑ Quarter Moon Books & Gifts: Topsail Beach
- ❑ Random Excitement and Adventure Daily Books: Marion
- ❑ Read'em & Weep: Grandy
- ❑ Read with Me: A Children's Book & Art Shop: Raleigh
- ❑ Sassafras on Sutton: Black Mountain
- ❑ Scuppernong Books: Greensboro
- ❑ Scuttlebutt: Nautical Books & Bounty: Beaufort
- ❑ Shakespeare and Company Bookseller: Highlands
- ❑ Shelves Bookstore: Charlotte
- ❑ South Main Book Company: Salisbury
- ❑ Sunrise Books: High Point
- ❑ The Book Shelf: Tryon
- ❑ The Coffee Hound Book Shop: Louisburg
- ❑ The Country Bookshop: Southern Pines
- ❑ The Gothic Bookshop: Durham
- ❑ The Island Bookstore: Corolla, Duck, Kitty Hawk
- ❑ The Regulator Bookshop: Durham
- ❑ Two Sisters Bookery: Wilmington
- ❑ Unlimited Books for Kids: Franklin
- ❑ Walls of Books: Cornelius
- ❑ Wonderland Bookshop: Greensboro

Thomas Wolfe Memorial

Ext. 5567

52 N. Market St., Asheville, NC 28801

INTERVIEWS WITH NORTH CAROLINA BOOKSTORES

Ext. 8936

Listen to stories from some of our favorite bookshops in North Carolina.

 To hear any of these stories, dial 774-325-0503 and dial the four-digit extension.

North Dakota

Apple in the Middle by Dawn Quigley 8442
Three Women by Lisa Taddeo..................................5929

NORTH DAKOTA BOOKSTORES

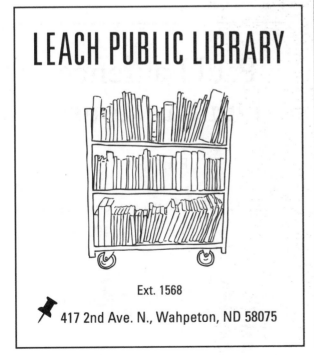

- ❑ Books on Broadway: Williston
- ❑ Ferguson Books & More!: Bismarck, Grand Forks
- ❑ Main Street Books: Minot
- ❑ Sweets 'N Stories: Oakes

LEACH PUBLIC LIBRARY

Ext. 1568

417 2nd Ave. N., Wahpeton, ND 58075

INTERVIEWS WITH NORTH DAKOTA BOOKSTORES

Ext. 4937

Listen to stories from some of our favorite bookshops in North Dakota.

Oceans

Atlantic by Simon Winchester.................................5984
Counting Descent by Clint Smith.............................3482
Dear America: Voyage on the Great Titanic by Ellen Emerson White..6684
Moby-Dick by Herman Melville...............................3778
Smithsonian Handbooks: Shells by S. Peter Dance 1814
The Awakening by Kate Chopin..............................2835
The Bell Jar by Sylvia Plath......................................4465
The Old Man and the Sea by Ernest Hemingway 5349

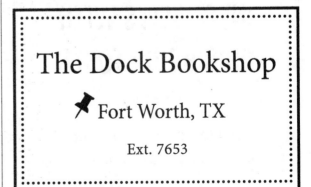

The Dock Bookshop

Fort Worth, TX

Ext. 7653

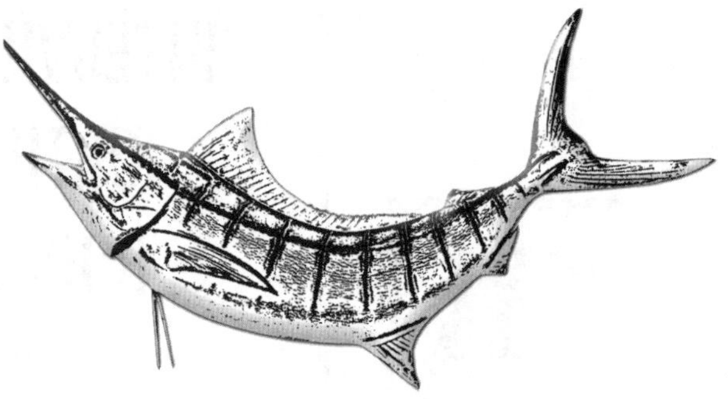

Marlin Fishing Tours

We'll put you over the fish all day!

Call Santiago: 5349

Ohio

INTERVIEWS WITH OHIO BOOKSTORES

Ext. 6934

Listen to stories from some of our favorite bookshops in Ohio.

Paul Laurence Dunbar House

Ext. 9838

219 N. Paul Laurence Dunbar St.
Dayton, OH 45402

 To hear any of these stories, dial 774-325-0503 and dial the four-digit extension.

OHIO BOOKSTORES

- ❑ A Cultural Exchange: Cleveland
- ❑ Appletree Books: Cleveland Heights
- ❑ Beanbag Books: Delaware
- ❑ Blue Manatee Literacy Project Bookstore: Cincinnati
- ❑ Books 'N' More: Wilmington
- ❑ Books of Aurora: Aurora
- ❑ Books Tell You Why: Columbus
- ❑ Browse Awhile Books: Tipp City
- ❑ BW Bookstore: Berea
- ❑ Cover to Cover Books for Young Readers: Columbus
- ❑ Downbound Books: Cincinnati
- ❑ Elizabeth's Bookshop & Writing Center: Akron
- ❑ Fireside Book Shop: Chagrin Falls
- ❑ Florence O. Wilson Bookstore: Wooster
- ❑ Fox's Book Adventures: Logan
- ❑ Gathering Volumes: Perrysburg
- ❑ Gramercy Books: Bexley
- ❑ Half Price Books: Beavercreek, Cincinnati, Columbus, Hamilton, Mason, Mayfield Heights, Lewis Center, North Olmsted, Reynoldsburg, Westerville
- ❑ Inscribed Books & Gifts: Mariemont
- ❑ Jane Austen Books: Novelty
- ❑ Jay and Mary's Book Center: Troy
- ❑ Joseph-Beth Booksellers: Cincinnati
- ❑ KiCam Books & Gifts: Mt. Orab
- ❑ Kicks Mix Bookstore: Newark
- ❑ Library House Books and Art: Grand Rapids
- ❑ Little Professor Book Center: Athens
- ❑ Loganberry Books: Shaker Heights
- ❑ Logos Bookstore: Kent
- ❑ Mac's Backs: Cleveland Heights
- ❑ Maia's Books & Misc.: Columbus
- ❑ Main Street Books: Mansfield
- ❑ MindFair Books: Oberlin
- ❑ Murphy's Used Books & Media: Kettering
- ❑ New & Olde Pages Book Shoppe: Englewood
- ❑ Once Upon a Thyme Bookshop: Beavercreek
- ❑ Paperback Shack: Niles
- ❑ Paragraphs Bookstore: Mt. Vernon
- ❑ Prologue Bookshop: Columbus
- ❑ Red Letter Days: Kent
- ❑ Smarty Pants: Findlay
- ❑ Smith & Hannon Book Store: Cincinnati
- ❑ Snowball Bookshop: Barberton
- ❑ St. Raphael Bookstore: Canton
- ❑ The Book Loft of German Village: Columbus
- ❑ The Book Rack: Cincinnati
- ❑ The Booksellers on Fountain Square: Cincinnati
- ❑ The Bookshelf: Cincinnati
- ❑ The Bookshelf: Medina
- ❑ The Bookshop in Lakewood: Lakewood
- ❑ The Fine Print: Lakeside
- ❑ The Learned Owl Book Shop: Hudson
- ❑ Two Dollar Radio Headquarters: Columbus
- ❑ Wheatberry Books: Chillicothe

Oklahoma

Outsiders House Museum

Ext. 7803

731 N. St. Louis Ave., Tulsa, OK 74106

Sequoyah's Cabin Museum

Ext. 1569

470288 Hwy. 101, Sallisaw, OK 74955

OKLAHOMA BOOKSTORES

- ❑ Best of Books: Edmond
- ❑ Bliss Books & Bindery: Stillwater
- ❑ Brace Books & More: Ponca City
- ❑ Chapters: Miami
- ❑ Full Circle Bookstore: Oklahoma City
- ❑ Fulton Street Books & Coffee: Tulsa
- ❑ Gardner's Used Books and Music: Tulsa
- ❑ Half Price Books: Edmond, Oklahoma City
- ❑ Lavender's Bleu Literacy Market: Tulsa
- ❑ Magic City Books: Tulsa
- ❑ Mocha Books: Tulsa
- ❑ PennWell Books: Tulsa
- ❑ The Book Exchange & Bible Bookstore: Pryor
- ❑ The Bookseller: Ardmore
- ❑ Tulsa Toy Depot: Tulsa
- ❑ Whirlwind Book Bar: Altus

Old Copies

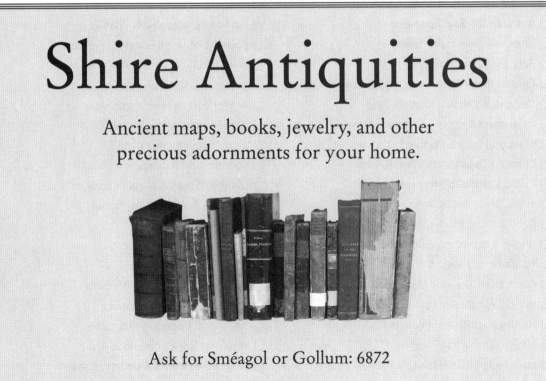

Oregon

Downwind from Nobody by Joan Wells....................7692
Girl by Blake Nelson 8721
One Flew Over the Cuckoo's Nest by Ken Kesey 8633

Page-turners

1984 by George Orwell..1984
American Psycho by Bret Easton Ellis 4657
House of Leaves by Mark Z. Danielewski.................4625

OREGON BOOKSTORES

- ❑ A Children's Place: Portland
- ❑ Annie Bloom's Books: Portland
- ❑ Another Read Through: Portland
- ❑ Beach Books: Seaside
- ❑ Betty's Books: Baker City
- ❑ Bloomsbury Books: Ashland
- ❑ Bob's Beach Books: Lincoln City
- ❑ Books Around the Corner: Gresham
- ❑ Books by the Bay: North Bend
- ❑ Broadway Books: Portland
- ❑ Bulk Bookstore: Portland
- ❑ Cannon Beach Book Company: Cannon Beach
- ❑ Canvasback Books: Klamath Falls
- ❑ Castlemere Books for Children: Astoria
- ❑ Chaparral Books: Portland
- ❑ Chapters Books and Coffee: Newberg
- ❑ Cloud & Leaf Bookstore: Manzanita
- ❑ Cross Genre Books: West Linn
- ❑ Daedalus Books: Portland
- ❑ Dudley's Bookshop Cafe: Bend
- ❑ Godfather's Books: Astoria
- ❑ Grass Roots Books & Music: Corvallis
- ❑ Green Bean Books: Portland
- ❑ Herringbone Books: Redmond
- ❑ J. Michaels Books: Eugene
- ❑ Jan's Paperbacks: Aloha
- ❑ Kinokuniya: Beaverton
- ❑ Klindt's Booksellers: The Dalles
- ❑ Lucy's Books: Astoria
- ❑ Maggie Mae's Kids Bookshop: Gresham
- ❑ Microcosm Publishing's Bookstory: Portland
- ❑ MudPuddles Toys & Books: Sherwood
- ❑ North by Northwest Books & Antiques: Lincoln City
- ❑ Oregon Books & Games: Grants Pass
- ❑ Paulina Springs Books: Sisters
- ❑ Powell's Books: Beaverton, Portland
- ❑ Powell's City of Books: Portland
- ❑ Reader's Guide: Salem
- ❑ Rebel Heart Books: Jacksonville
- ❑ Robert's Bookshop: Lincoln City
- ❑ Roundabout Books: Bend
- ❑ Soundpeace: Ashland
- ❑ Sunriver Books & Music: Sunriver
- ❑ The Book Bin: Corvallis, Salem
- ❑ The Book Nook: Canby
- ❑ The Bookloft: Enterprise
- ❑ The Open Book: Bend
- ❑ Third Street Books: McMinnville
- ❑ Tree House Books: Ashland
- ❑ Two Rivers Bookstore: Portland
- ❑ Waucoma Bookstore: Hood River
- ❑ WinterRiver Books & Gallery: Bandon

Beverly Cleary Sculpture Garden

Ext. 9355

Grant Park Path, Portland, OR 97212

Turning Page Bookshop

Goose Creek, SC

Ext. 7804

In the Kingdom of Ice by Hampton Sides 7742
In the Woods by Tana French..................................7743
The Glass Bead Game by Hermann Hesse 7818
The Hot Zone by Richard Preston 6873

Parenting

Amelia Frump and Her Peanut Butter Loving, Overactive Imagination Is Cooking Up a Peanut Butter Storm by Debbie Roppolo 2798

INTERVIEWS WITH OREGON BOOKSTORES

Ext. 8500

Listen to stories from some of our favorite bookshops in Oregon.

Dandelion Wine by Ray Bradbury............................4601
Far from the Tree by Andrew Solomon.....................9422
Not Even Wrong by Paul Collins...............................6802
Short Order Dad by Robert Rosenthal.......................1815
Stranger in a Strange Land by Robert A. Heinlein....1828
The Grapes of Wrath by John Steinbeck 6864

Call about the memorable book you read to your children (or can't wait to read to a child soon).

774-325-0503

Ext. 3499

The Wind in the Willows by Kenneth Grahame 2582
Their Eyes Were Watching God by
Zora Neale Hurston 6924

An anonymous voicemail message about

Dandelion Wine by Ray Bradbury

Ext. 4601

Hi, Ishmael. I wanted to call you and talk to you about a book called *Dandelion Wine* by Ray Bradbury. It isn't really like other books; it's more of a fictional account of his own childhood. I like it because, before I had kids, I imagined daughters. I imagined being this magical mom, like my mom was to me. But then I had sons, and I was really scared. For some reason, I felt like I didn't know how to . . . I don't know, be magic to boys. And for them, I read *Dandelion Wine*. My copy was used and beat-up and it smelled like old paperback books do, which is like honestly the best smell in the world. But anyway, *Dandelion Wine* became the closest thing that I found to a book about how I want to parent. It's not like a how-to book or expert book about parenting, but it's really just about the simple magic of leaving your kids alone with their minds and their imagination and their neighborhood and their adventures and giving them the space for that—the space to build a happiness machine, like they do in the book. Or to bottle up summer like dandelion wine. And space to learn, like that they're faster with new shoes. The book's a little bit like *Tom Sawyer* and a little bit of, like, a simpler time. But it's a whole lot of remembering what is really important, and that maybe the magic part is that my boys already are the magic. I'm just along for the ride. So. That's *Dandelion Wine*. Thanks for being there, Ishmael. We sure appreciate you. Bye. ☎

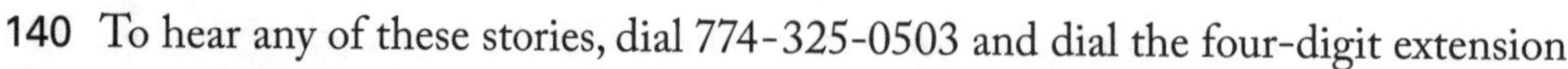

Pennsylvania

August Wilson Childhood Home

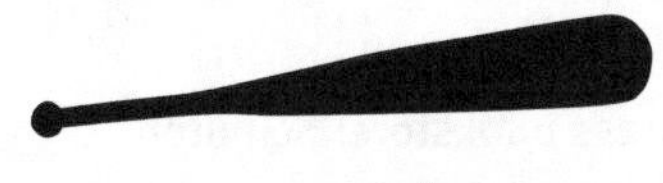

Ext. 7357

1727 Bedford Ave.
Pittsburgh, PA 15219

INTERVIEWS WITH PENNSYLVANIA BOOKSTORES

Ext. 8799

Listen to stories from some of our favorite bookshops in Pennsylvania.

Dickens and Little Nell Statue

Ext. 9356

4301 Chester Ave., Philadelphia, PA 19104

PENNSYLVANIA BOOKSTORES

- ❑ A Novel Idea: Philadelphia
- ❑ Aaron's Books: Lititz
- ❑ Adamstown Books: Lancaster
- ❑ B. R. Books: Lancaster
- ❑ Baldwin's Book Barn: West Chester
- ❑ Big Blue Marble Bookstore: Philadelphia
- ❑ Book & Puppet Company: Easton
- ❑ Books Upstairs: Bath
- ❑ Bradley's Book Outlet: Altoona, Cranberry, DuBois, Grove City, Indiana, Pittsburgh, State College, Tarentum, Uniontown
- ❑ Carroll & Carroll Booksellers: Stroudsburg
- ❑ Children's Book World: Haverford
- ❑ City of Asylum Bookstore: Pittsburgh
- ❑ Classic Lines: Pittsburgh
- ❑ Commonplace Reader: Yardley
- ❑ Completely Booked: Murrysville
- ❑ Cupboard Maker Books: Enola
- ❑ Detecto Mysterioso: Philadelphia
- ❑ Farley's Bookshop: New Hope
- ❑ Firefly Bookstore: Kutztown
- ❑ From My Shelf Books & Gifts: Wellsboro
- ❑ Half Price Books: Bethel Park, Monroeville, Pittsburgh
- ❑ Harriet's Bookshop: Philadelphia
- ❑ Head House Books: Philadelphia
- ❑ Heisenbooks: Fairless Hills
- ❑ House of Our Own: Philadelphia
- ❑ Ideas Bookstore: Phoenixville
- ❑ JaZams: Lahaska
- ❑ Jewish Kids Bookstore: Moosic
- ❑ Joseph Fox Bookshop: Philadelphia
- ❑ Lahaska Bookshop: Lahaska
- ❑ Leana's Books and More: Grove City, Hermitage
- ❑ Let's Play Books!: Emmaus
- ❑ Library Express Bookstore: Scranton
- ❑ Little Green Bookshop: Cresco
- ❑ Main Point Books: Wayne
- ❑ Mechanicsburg Mystery Bookshop: Mechanicsburg
- ❑ Midtown Scholar Bookstore: Harrisburg
- ❑ Mystery Lovers Bookshop: Oakmont
- ❑ Narberth Bookshop: Narberth
- ❑ Newtown Bookshop: Newtown
- ❑ On the Side Books: Bradford
- ❑ Open Book Bookstore: Elkins Park
- ❑ Otto Bookstore: Williamsport
- ❑ Penguin Bookshop: Sewickley
- ❑ People's Books & Culture: Philadelphia
- ❑ Philly AIDS Thrift @ Giovanni's Room: Philadelphia
- ❑ Pilothouse Nautical Books and Charts: Philadelphia
- ❑ Pressed: Erie
- ❑ Prosperity Bookstore: Philadelphia
- ❑ Reads & Company: Phoenixville
- ❑ Rickert & Beagle Books: Pittsburgh
- ❑ Riverstone Books: Pittsburgh
- ❑ Second Chapter Books: Ligonier

PENNSYLVANIA BOOKSTORES (CONT.)

- ❑ Shakespeare & Co.: Philadelphia
- ❑ Spark Books: Aspinwall
- ❑ Starr Books: Douglassville
- ❑ Tattered Corners New and Used Bookstore: Meadville
- ❑ The Book Nook: Boyertown
- ❑ The Caffeinated Bookworm: Lancaster
- ❑ The Crooked Shelf Bookshop: Lewistown
- ❑ The Doylestown Bookshop: Doylestown
- ❑ The Spiral Bookcase: Philadelphia
- ❑ The Tiny Bookstore: Pittsburgh
- ❑ Uncle Bobbie's Coffee and Books: Philadelphia
- ❑ Wellington Square Bookshop: Exton
- ❑ Werner Books: Erie
- ❑ Whistlestop Bookshop: Carlisle
- ❑ White Whale Bookstore: Pittsburgh

Pets

A Dog's Purpose by W. Bruce Cameron 3120
Dogsbody by Diana Wynne Jones 7690
Good Dog, Carl by Alexandra Day 8723
Strawberry Fields by Marina Lewycka 2830

Lenny's Pet Shop

Ext. 2234

Call me Fishmael?

Text us a pic of your pets named for literary greats. We'll share them on @callingishmael.

Text photos:
774-325-0503

Wild Rumpus

Old Saybrook, CT

Ext. 7653

The Call of the Wild by Jack London 4938
The Friend by Sigrid Nunez 6857

Pigs

A Normal Pig by K-Fai Steele 2647
Animal Farm by George Orwell 1029
Charlotte's Web by E. B. White 7565
I Like Me! by Nancy Carlson 5001
Olivia by Ian Falconer 3790
Serious Pig by John Thorne 1114

Prank Calls

Con Air by Simon West 4433
Forrest Gump by Winston Groom 2437
The Lorax by Dr. Seuss 1962

Flying Pig Bookstore

Ext. 8881

Napoleon's Meats

Cold cuts! BBQ! Bacon!

Call: 1029

Public Transit

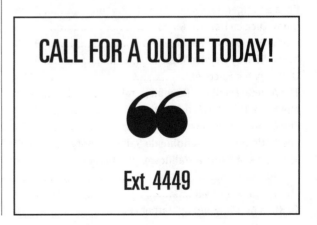

Quotable

The Library Book by Susan Orlean 4444
The Little Prince by Antoine de Saint-Exupéry.........7777
The Notebook by Nicholas Sparks...........................7887
The Parrot's Lament by Eugene Linden 7892
The Stranger by Albert Camus 7917
Their Eyes Were Watching God by
Zora Neale Hurston 5927
Wool by Hugh Howey...4604

Read Slowly

Bury My Heart at Wounded Knee by Dee Brown 4778
Dandelion Wine by Ray Bradbury............................6683
Ready Player One by Ernest Cline 2235
The Giver by Lois Lowry 5854
The Oldest Living Things in the World by
Rachel Sussman 7563

Reading Out Loud

A Wrinkle in Time by Madeleine L'Engle..................2359
A Year Down Yonder by Richard Peck.......................3649
Brown Bear, Brown Bear, What Do You See?
by Bill Martin 5675
Dinnertime by Jan Pieńkowski 4592
Ender's Game by Orson Scott Card 7695
Flip, Flap, Fly!: A Book for Babies Everywhere
by Phyllis Root...7338
Harry Potter and the Sorcerer's Stone by
J. K. Rowling...8728
Harry Potter series by J. K. Rowling.........................6342
I'm a Stranger Here Myself by Bill Bryson 7738
Moby-Dick by Herman Melville...............................1980
Moby-Dick by Herman Melville...............................3780
Moby-Dick by Herman Melville...............................4777
Olivia by Ian Falconer 3790
The Animal Family by Randall Jarrell 5491
The Book Thief by Markus Zusak............................2837
The Giver by Lois Lowry 5854
The Little Prince by Antoine de Saint-Exupéry.........3223
The Perks of Being a Wallflower by Stephen
Chbosky 7807
Thirst by Mary Oliver 1003
To Kill a Mockingbird by Harper Lee........................1964
Tuesdays with Morrie by Mitch Albom 6000
Watership Down by Richard Adams 9834

An anonymous voicemail message about

Thirst by Mary Oliver

Ext. 1003

Hi, Ishmael. I want to tell you about a book I love called *Thirst*, a book of poetry by Mary Oliver. One of my very best friends and I both fell in love with this book. We had talked about a number of books together, including another book called *An Altar in the World*. Not poetry, but full of wisdom. One of the points in this book is to read poetry to trees. The author talks about how this is a really healthy habit. I know that's really unexpected. But I used the book *Thirst* with my friend Megan to serenade the trees of Sevier Park in Nashville, Tennessee. We chose some of our favorite poems from that book, "Messenger," and, of course, "When I Am Among the Trees" to read to some of the trees that looked like they needed a little extra water, and really had a great time. A lot of people looked on with perplexed looks, but we continued and it was a really special day. Kind of liberating. "Among the Trees" spoke to me in a more profound way because I actually read poetry to trees as I was among them. Okay, thanks, Ishmael. I appreciate your letting me tell my story and I will talk to you later. Bye. ☎

Tuesday Reading Series

Life lessons from live readings, weekly

Call Mitch to RSVP: 6000

Leave a message about a book someone once read out loud to you.

Ext. 8800

Reading Rainbow

From the Mixed-Up Files of Mrs. Basil E. Frankweiler by E. L. Konigsburg 1024
Green Eggs and Ham by Dr. Seuss 4614
Little Women by Louisa May Alcott..........................1039
The Berenstain Bears' New Baby by Stan and Jan Berenstain 2838
The Littles to the Rescue by John Peterson..............6879
The Secret Garden by Frances Hodgson Burnett 9903
The Velveteen Rabbit by Margery Williams..............6920

Reading Slump

Do Androids Dream of Electric Sheep? by Philip K. Dick 7688
Let's Pretend This Never Happened by Jenny Lawson..5760
Not in God's Name by Jonathan Sacks 3784

'N' Sip It

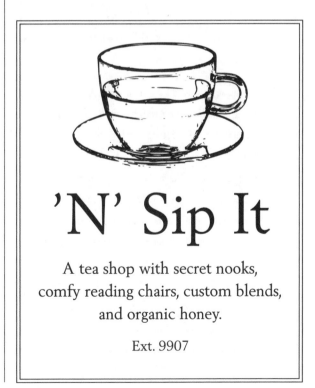

A tea shop with secret nooks, comfy reading chairs, custom blends, and organic honey.

Ext. 9907

The Eye of the World series by Robert Jordan..........4351
The Secret Life of Bees by Sue Monk Kidd..............9907

Religion

American Gods by Neil Gaiman..............................3655
God Is Disappointed in You by Mark Russell...........8718
Good Omens by Neil Gaiman and Terry Pratchett....1370
He, She and It by Marge Piercy.............................1812
Inherit the Wind by Jerome Lawrence and Robert E. Lee..9327
Living Buddha, Living Christ by Thich Nhat Hanh..4587
Maus by Art Spiegelman.......................................4454
Not in God's Name by Jonathan Sacks....................3784
Of Human Bondage by W. Somerset Maugham.......3791

An anonymous voicemail message about

Living Buddha, Living Christ by Thich Nhat Hanh

Ext. 4587

Hey, Ishmael. I guess I want to start this off by saying that I'm not a religious person—I'm probably more spiritual than religious—but the book that has changed my life the most is *Living Buddha, Living Christ* by Thich Nhat Hanh. I guess in a way, like all early twentysomethings-slash-teenagers, I went through my period of depression. I was living in London at the time, away from my family, and just couldn't handle the pressure, and was just way in over my head and would isolate myself from everyone and not live like I wanted to. And I found this book. It was actually given to me by my father, inscribed with a note to me about reading and appreciating, and that was it. I knew that it was changing my life when I started writing down the quotes that stuck with me. In classes, whenever I was feeling overwhelmed, I would go back to these quotes and keep reading them and reading them in my head, including "To breathe and know you're alive is wonderful. Because you are alive, everything is possible," and "Don't waste a single moment." "The miracle is not to walk on water. The miracle is to walk on the green earth and be present in the moment." Since this book, I've really been trying to live that as my mantra: to be present, to be aware, to feel the energy with everybody and let myself live and let myself struggle and let myself be. This book is just mind-blowingly incredible. And that's all I have to say. ☎

Remedies

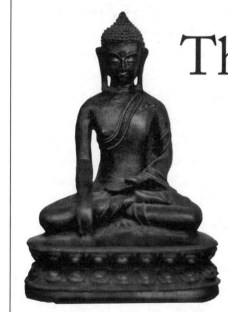

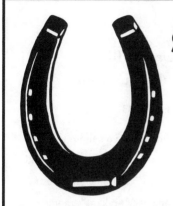

Required Reading

Re-Readable

An anonymous voicemail message about

Norwegian Wood by Haruki Murakami

Ext. 3783

Hi, Ishmael. I want to talk to you about the first book to really break my heart, which was Haruki Murakami's *Norwegian Wood*. *Norwegian Wood* is considered to be one of Murakami's more traditional stories, so the magical realism is really toned down here, but it's about nineteen-year-old Toru, who in his early years of college finds himself falling in love with two women, the bright eccentric Naoko, and Midori, who is his dead best friend's girl. I think even Murakami's admitted that the basic premise of a love triangle is a little cliché, but there's a really pervasive sense of loss and heartbreak, so it's a story that kind of grabs you and refuses to let go. I first read this novel when I was around sixteen years old, and I think a part of me's been stuck there ever since. Seeing these characters trying to understand each other while barely understanding themselves really resonated with me in a way that I'd never seen before. I reread *Norwegian Wood* this year, and I'm now twenty-two, and it was a completely different experience. When I first read it, I was looking towards the future and wondering who I'd become once I moved away from home and started university. But rereading it this year, I found myself looking back to those vulnerable first years alone, to

 To hear any of these stories, dial 774-325-0503 and dial the four-digit extension.

really baring your heart and soul for the first time. I was blown away by how many of the conversations in the novel were actually ones that I've since had. I realize I'm still very young and the idea of a twenty-two-year-old looking back with nostalgia may be a little bit laughable, but it amazes me how much one story can change with just the right amount of time. I think I'll make *Norwegian Wood* a once-in-a-decade thing, read it in my thirties, forties, and onward. I'm kind of looking forward to seeing how the novel and I will change then. Thank you. ☎

The Chronicles of Narnia series by C. S. Lewis 4593
The Crying of Lot 49 by Thomas Pynchon 4849
The Dogs of Babel by Carolyn Parkhurst 7689
The Giver by Lois Lowry 6858
The God of Small Things by Arundhati Roy..............6862
The Mother-Daughter Book Club by Heather Vogel Frederick 7883
The Particular Sadness of Lemon Cake by Aimee Bender 7889
The Power by Naomi Alderman 8895

Read It Again

Suwanee, GA

Ext. 2228

The Stranger by Albert Camus 4626
To Kill a Mockingbird by Harper Lee 1964
Watership Down by Richard Adams 9834
Words in Air by Elizabeth Bishop and Robert Lowell..2955
Yes Please by Amy Poehler 3957

Rhode Island

The One and Only Ivan by Katherine Applegate 1122
Three Women by Lisa Taddeo.................................5929

INTERVIEWS WITH RHODE ISLAND BOOKSTORES

Ext. 3747

Listen to stories from some of our favorite bookshops in Rhode Island.

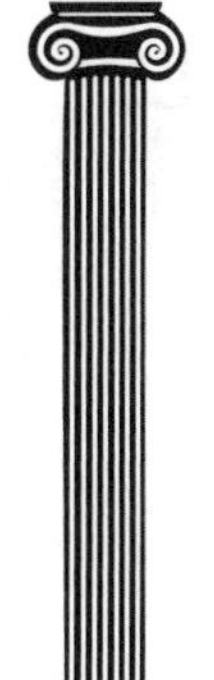

PROVIDENCE ATHENÆUM

Ext. 4158

251 Benefit St.
Providence, RI 02903

RHODE ISLAND BOOKSTORES

- ❑ Barrington Books: Barrington
- ❑ Barrington Books Retold: Cranston
- ❑ Books on the Pond: Charlestown
- ❑ Books on the Square: Providence
- ❑ Ink Fish Books: Warren
- ❑ Island Books: Middletown
- ❑ Island Bound Bookstore: Block Island
- ❑ Riffraff: Providence
- ❑ Savoy Bookshop & Café: Westerly
- ❑ Spring Street Bookstore: Newport
- ❑ Symposium Books: Providence
- ❑ The Book Nerd: Barrington
- ❑ The Collective: South Kingstown
- ❑ Wakefield Books: Wakefield

Ruined Copies/Ruined Books

Moby-Dick by Herman Melville.................................1980
Sharp Objects by Gillian Flynn................................8777

LEAVE A MESSAGE ABOUT THE STRANGEST THING YOU EVER FOUND IN A BOOK.

774-325-0503

Ext. 1157

Song of Solomon by Toni Morrison 9939
Texfake by W. Thomas Taylor..................................1005

Saving the World

Ishmael by Daniel Quinn 1035
Ishmael by Daniel Quinn 6170
Ishmael by Daniel Quinn 6752
Miss Rumphius by Barbara Cooney.........................8332
The Hobbit by J. R. R. Tolkien 6872

"Teacher seeks pupil. Must have an earnest desire to save the world. Apply in person."

Ext. 6170

 To hear any of these stories, dial 774-325-0503 and dial the four-digit extension.

You could spend half your life browsing our massive collection of science lab materials.

Closed periodically: 7203

Science

A Short History of Nearly Everything by Bill Bryson 7722
Fundamental Formulas of Physics edited by Donald H. Menzel 7555
On Looking by Alexandra Horowitz 4599
Smithsonian Handbooks: Shells by S. Peter Dance 1814

An anonymous voicemail message about

A Short History of Nearly Everything
by Bill Bryson

Ext. 7722

Hi, Ishmael. I'm calling in response to Joe Hanson's request for a book that changed how you feel about and see the natural world. The book that single-handedly altered the vista through which I see everything is Bill Bryson's *A Short History of Nearly Everything*. It covers everything from corks to quasars, from the trained scientist to the happenstance experimenter. It rekindled in me a yearning passion for science by showing me how significant and how insignificant I am. Before reading this, I kind of wrote chemistry off as stamp collecting and biology off as a dormant science. But now I not only see the interconnectedness of these fields, but also how alive they are. I think it's a shame for anyone on this planet to misunderstand the scientific process. This book is both thorough and approachable and its history is deeply introspective yet lighthearted. It reminds me how science isn't just an ideology to be written off. It's a practice, an art form still budding in its years. After reading this book, I feel that science has something far more beautiful than anything else this universe has to offer: an explanation. ☎

The Elements by Theodore Gray............................7203
The Hot Zone by Richard Preston 6873
The Immortal Life of Henrietta Lacks by
Rebecca Skloot...4960
The Martian by Andy Weir......................................1051

Seeing Yourself in a Book

A Thousand Acres by Jane Smiley 2113
Alice's Adventures in Wonderland by
Lewis Carroll..3652
American Born Chinese by Gene Luen Yang 1025
Born on a Blue Day by Daniel Tammet....................1981
Cassandra at the Wedding by Dorothy Baker 3323
Cut by Patricia McCormick 7810
Epileptic by David B. 8700
Esperanza Rising by Pam Muñoz Ryan 8701
I Am the Darker Brother edited by Arnold Adoff 2368
In the Time of the Butterflies by Julia Alvarez 8000
Ishmael by Daniel Quinn 6752
Keeping You a Secret by Julie Anne Peters 8630
Matilda by Roald Dahl 9837
One Flew Over the Cuckoo's Nest by Ken Kesey 8633
The Book Thief by Markus Zusak............................1007
The Diary of a Young Girl by Anne Frank..................2035
The Fellowship of the Ring by J. R. R. Tolkien...........1976
The House on Mango Street by Sandra Cisneros.....8864
The House on Mango Street by Sandra Cisneros.....9325
The Joy Luck Club by Amy Tan 7749
The Namesake by Jhumpa Lahiri............................7886
The Summer I Turned Pretty by Jenny Han..............4931
Tiger Eyes by Judy Blume......................................3046
Twilight by Stephenie Meyer 6668
What's Left of Me by Kat Zhang..............................1949
Where the Stars Still Shine by Trish Doller.............1301

Self-Love

Cornelia and the Audacious Escapades of the
Somerset Sisters by Lesley M. M. Blume............7817
Escape from Asylum by Madeleine Roux.................1982
Figuring by Maria Popova 9711
Franny and Zooey by J. D. Salinger.........................4608
Harry Potter series by J. K. Rowling.........................7561
I Am Not Myself These Days by
Josh Kilmer-Purcell 5986

Dr. Eckleburg Eye Exams
Hindsight is 20/20!
Call for appointment: 6865

An anonymous voicemail message about

The Joy Luck Club by Amy Tan

Ext. 7749

The minute I picked up *The Joy Luck Club* was the first time I saw myself represented in a novel. I'm an Asian American woman growing up in the United States. My parents are immigrants from the Philippines, and I don't fully understand a lot of the sacrifices they made to come to the United States. Both my grandmothers survived World War II, and horrifically the Japanese took over their homes and then their land. And Amy Tan, she examines the pain that immigrants go through. Representation is very important in novels and we don't really see it very often. It's typically white males or white females. She really portrayed an Asian family in a beautiful light, and it helped me understand my family in a multigenerational way: through my grandmother, through my mom, and then through my father. Sometimes we feel like we can't relate to our parents or relate to our grandparents, but if we really sit down and listen to their stories we can understand their sufferings. Amy Tan really brings that to light. So thanks, Ishmael. ☎

An anonymous voicemail message about

Never Let Me Go by Kazuo Ishiguro

Ext. 3789

Hi, Ishmael. I'm going to try really hard not to break into tears while I do this—okay, here we go. The novel I want to talk to you about is called *Never Let Me Go* by Kazuo Ishiguro. And I don't want to tell you about the plot of the book because that's not really what I'm here for. I want to tell you about the feeling. In the book, there's this girl and she lives in this world where everyone sacrifices themselves. Not as a sign of strength or courage or to be any sort of Superman in anyone's eyes. Everyone sacrifices themselves; it's just what they do. People give up their loves and their passions and everything that makes them bother to get up in the morning just for the hope of maybe a passing smile. A quiet thank you. Something to say it was worth it. And I . . . I guess it's not. Because in this book it's not about giving up dance or drama or writing or fishing. Everyone is giving up themselves. They're giving up arms and legs and stomachs and kidneys and even hearts, and nobody bothers to say thank you. No one even looks at those people in the eye. And it, it kind of gets to the point in the book where they start to wonder if they're even human at all really. Because what sort of person does that? What sort of person offers themselves up in that way? It's cruel, really, almost begging to be taken advantage of. And gets taken advantage of. There's this passage in the book that goes, "Maybe, in a way, we didn't leave it behind nearly as much as we might once have thought. Because somewhere underneath, a part of us stayed like that: fearful of the world around us, and—no matter how much we despised ourselves for it—unable quite to let each other go." When I was reading that book for the first time—maybe because it was four a.m.—but I knew that passage was me. One hundred percent me. Because every day up until then, and sometimes still now, I try to give up parts of myself, parts I don't like—some snark here, a rude comment there. Anything that makes me myself. And I like to pretend that it's because I'm really brave, training myself to become who I ideally want to be, but I think maybe it's not because of that. I'm changing myself because I'm just terrified of who I really am. And the book *Never Let Me Go* ironically taught me to let myself go. To try to live as I am and not as others want me to be—which for someone who's so self-conscious and self-hating and just completely against their own selves by nature is almost impossible. But it happened. It happened because of twenty-six letters arranged into a book. And that book is *Never Let Me Go*. Thank you. ☎

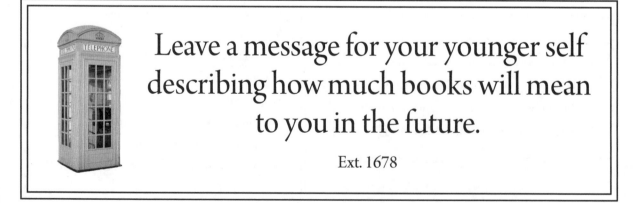

I Like Me! by Nancy Carlson 5001
I'm with the Band by Pamela Des Barres................7739
Icy Sparks by Gwyn Hyman Rubio 7740
Invisible Man by Ralph Ellison 5348
Kushiel's Dart by Jacqueline Carey 5756
Never Let Me Go by Kazuo Ishiguro.........................3789
Queen Know Your Worth by Rashanda Crisp 2806
Sex Criminals by Matt Fraction and Chip Zdarsky....7838
Stargirl by Jerry Spinelli...1009
Sula by Toni Morrison 1826
The Tightrope Walker by Dorothy Gilman 7918

Leave a message for your younger self describing how much books will mean to you in the future.

Ext. 1678

Serendipity

An anonymous voicemail message about

A Little Life
by Hanya Yanagihara

Ext. 2643

About a year after moving from New York to San Francisco, my manager at work asked if I could help with a rather exceptional customer. He was visiting from Seoul and needed assistance in traveling to a remote address in Berkeley. He neither spoke nor understood much English. He was, however, remarkably patient, and after a good deal of creative communication we succeeded in setting up a map on his phone, as well as personal accounts with Uber and Lyft. Despite our language barrier—or perhaps because of it—we connected quite a bit throughout the process. When my work was done, though, I could by no means have anticipated the level of gratitude that poured from his heart. He thanked me countless times, shaking my hand with great vigor while requesting a picture together. We parted ways with a sense of newfound friendship. Not long after, I picked up a copy of *A Little Life*, Hanya Yanagihara's novel that also deals with friendship. For reasons both expected and incomprehensible, the story cast on me a deep spell, and each day thereafter I found myself engrossed in it for hours on end. To cope with its more traumatizing moments, I read while wandering San Francisco's many neighborhoods, an experience that in some sense paralleled the story's own traversal of neighborhoods in New York. Most of the novel centers around Lispenard Street, a little corridor in Downtown Manhattan. I was visiting New York last month, and having finished the novel decided to lend it to a friend who worked at the World Trade Center. I realized Lispenard Street was not so far away, and decided to take a little detour and pay homage to one of the story's great epicenters. Just past Canal, I spied Lispenard Street. Pausing beneath its sign, I felt a small stream of clarity flow through me, as though something about Yanagihara's captivating and mysterious story had at once settled in this space. Only in that moment did I hear my name, and I turned my head to see the man from Seoul staring at me with wide eyes and an open mouth, a look of disbelief and beauty shining across his face.

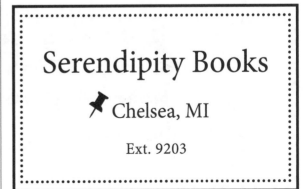

Serendipity Books

Chelsea, MI

Ext. 9203

Short Books

A Monster Calls by Patrick Ness..............................2646
Convenience Store Woman by Sayaka Murata.........6682
Dandelion Wine by Ray Bradbury............................7571
The Little Prince by Antoine de Saint-Exupéry.........7777
The Selection by Kiera Cass...................................7819
Tomorrow by Bradley Trevor Greive.........................4934
Wave by Sonali Deraniyagala.................................2944

Shyness

Horton Hears a Who! by Dr. Seuss 8732
I Am the Messenger by Markus Zusak.....................3842

 To hear any of these stories, dial 774-325-0503 and dial the four-digit extension.

Siblings

A River Runs Through It by Norman Maclean 3648
Cycle of the Werewolf by Stephen King 2363
Divergent by Veronica Roth 7686
Epileptic by David B. 8700

Sister's Uptown

New York, NY

Ext. 6240

An anonymous voicemail message about

Tiny Beautiful Things by Cheryl Strayed

Ext. 6059

Hi, Ishmael. I would like to talk to you about *Tiny Beautiful Things* by Cheryl Strayed. So, I have three sisters, and I always thought of them as the most amazing, beautiful, intelligent people I would ever know—and I thought they felt the same way about me. A few years ago, I started abusing drugs to the point where it almost killed me, and my sisters didn't say anything. They didn't write. They didn't call. They didn't ask me to get help. Without the intervention of my friends, I probably would have died. So I got this book as a gift. *Tiny Beautiful Things.* It's a collection of advice columns, and the overall theme of it is that life isn't fair and it might not always go the way you want it to, but you have to build your own life raft and get through it. Because it's not fair to anybody else, either. It really helped change my way of thinking. The person who sent it to me was my younger sister. It didn't come with a big note or anything about my drug use or about how she was glad I was alive or anything, but it made me think maybe this book meant a lot to her because maybe she went through her own thing that I don't know anything about. Maybe she was so busy building her own life raft that she didn't have time to help me build mine. So maybe there's still hope. Thanks, Ishmael. ☎

Fangirl by Rainbow Rowell 9708
Franny and Zooey by J. D. Salinger 4608
Harry Potter and the Sorcerer's Stone by J. K. Rowling 8728
Moby-Dick by Herman Melville 1980
The Berenstain Bears' New Baby by Stan and Jan Berenstain 2838
The Catcher in the Rye by J. D. Salinger 6969
The Particular Sadness of Lemon Cake by Aimee Bender 7889
Tiny Beautiful Things by Cheryl Strayed 6059

South Carolina

The Secret Life of Bees by Sue Monk Kidd..............9907

Charleston Library Society

164 King St., Charleston, SC 29401

Ext. 7660

INTERVIEWS WITH SOUTH CAROLINA BOOKSTORES

Ext. 1158

Listen to stories from some of our favorite bookshops in South Carolina.

SOUTH CAROLINA BOOKSTORES

- ❑ Bacchus & Books: Charleston
- ❑ Blue Bicycle Books: Charleston
- ❑ Books and Brews: Charleston
- ❑ Books on Broad: Camden
- ❑ Burry Bookstore: Hartsville
- ❑ Buxton Books: Charleston
- ❑ Ed's Editions: West Columbia
- ❑ Edisto Island Bookstore: Edisto Island
- ❑ Fiction Addiction: Greenville
- ❑ Hub City Bookshop: Spartanburg
- ❑ Indigo Books: Johns Island
- ❑ Itinerant Literate Bookstop: Charleston
- ❑ Litchfield Books: Pawleys Island
- ❑ M. Judson Booksellers: Greenville
- ❑ Main Street Reads: Summerville
- ❑ My Sister's Books: Pawleys Island
- ❑ NeverMore Books: Beaufort
- ❑ Poor Richard's Booksellers: Easley
- ❑ Relentless Chapters Bookstore: Greenville
- ❑ Swift Books: Orangeburg
- ❑ Sylvia Barnhill Designs: Mt. Pleasant
- ❑ The Beaufort Bookstore: Beaufort
- ❑ The Emorej Group: North Augusta
- ❑ The Reading Warehouse: North Charleston
- ❑ The Storybook Shoppe: Bluffton
- ❑ Turning Page Bookshop: Goose Creek
- ❑ Waterfront Books: Georgetown

 To hear any of these stories, dial 774-325-0503 and dial the four-digit extension.

Poe's Tavern

Ext. 9030

2210 Middle St.
Sullivan's Island, SC 29482

INTERVIEWS WITH SOUTH DAKOTA BOOKSTORES

Ext. 4679

Listen to stories from some of our favorite bookshops in South Dakota.

South Dakota

Bury My Heart at Wounded Knee by Dee Brown 4778
The Lakota Way by Joseph M. Marshall III 1121

SOUTH DAKOTA BOOKSTORES

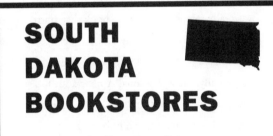

- Canyon Booksellers: Spearfish
- DDR Books: Watertown
- Mitzi's Books: Rapid City
- Prairie Pages Bookseller: Pierre
- Whimsy on Main: Milbank

Ingalls Homestead

Ext. 4159

20812 Homestead Rd., De Smet, SD 57231

Special Editions

American Born Chinese by Gene Luen Yang 1025
Little Women by Louisa May Alcott..........................1039
The Merchant of Venice by William Shakespeare 6882
The Spell Book of Listen Taylor by Jaclyn Moriarty....4600
The Wonderful Wizard of Oz by L. Frank Baum.........5926
To Kill a Mockingbird by Harper Lee.......................1964

An anonymous voicemail message about

American Born Chinese by Gene Luen Yang

Ext. 1025

It's by Gene Luen Yang and I believe it was the first graphic novel to ever win a Printz Award—which is really big—and I'm also fairly certain it's the first graphic novel to ever be nominated for a National Book Award. While those accolades are meaningful in a lot of ways for those who make graphic novels and read graphic novels, the thing about this particular book is that, this book *American Born Chinese*, it was really rare for me to see a book that starred Chinese characters in a way that was very real and in a really respectful way. Gene Luen Yang has actually said as National Ambassador for Young People's Literature that books should serve as both windows and mirrors. For the longest time, I haven't . . . I couldn't find a mirror, certainly not in my childhood. So, you know, as a woman in her twenties and thirties it was really, really refreshing to finally see that happen and to see it make way for more stories that allow for Asian American characters. On top of it all, it's just so beautifully illustrated and so remarkably weaves three story lines together, and I think it would introduce a lot of people to new mythology like the tale of the Monkey King. It's pretty amazing. I'm really happy actually to leave this message and to talk about his book and how much it meant to me and how much it still means to me, and how I'll always keep a copy—my copy of it that he autographed—in some plastic shrink-wrap, because that's how much I want to protect it and keep it forever. Bye. ☎

Sports

An anonymous voicemail message about

Fear and Loathing in Las Vegas by Hunter S. Thompson

Ext. 9709

Hey, Ishmael. When I was in college I read Hunter S. Thompson's *Fear and Loathing in Las Vegas* for the first time, and it was really an important experience for me for a lot of reasons. You know, I was kind of like a fledgling writer. I had just started, and in high school I had a football scholarship, and then I got injured my senior year, and I lost it. They took my scholarship away from me, so I couldn't go to college and play sports. I just remember being carted off the field and crying on a gurney, being taken to the hospital to get an MRI, and I remember saying, "My scholarship . . . My scholarship . . . It's over." 'Cause that was—that was my life. That's what my life was going to be. I was gonna go to the University of Oregon and I was going to play football and it was all decided. In this one moment—this one terribly unlucky moment, twisting the wrong way—you know, it completely changed things for me. A couple of days afterward, I was having a talk with my mom and told her I didn't know what to do. That I was feeling lost. I didn't even know if I wanted to go to college anymore. She reminded me that it had always been my goal, and it was true. I really wanted to go to school. But I didn't know what else to do other than football. That had been my thing. So she sat me down and she said, "Well, what else are you good at?" I started thinking about things and what classes I liked and I realized that I really liked my writing class. So I was like, "You know what? That's what I want to do. Let's do that." I really enjoyed it when we had to write creatively in class. We read a lot of, like, old white dudes in school, like Shakespeare and Hemingway—and I love Hemingway, but I couldn't see myself writing like that. I didn't know what kind of writer I could be and I was struggling with figuring that out. And then I read *Fear and Loathing in Las Vegas*. You know, I'm gonna be honest since you're a computer voicemail and I'll never meet you. I was partying a lot. Drugs and alcohol and whatnot. And here I read this book about a guy who's doing nothing but that, and he's a famous writer. He writes about [*laughs*] all this crazy stuff. So the book really got to me. And I—you know, I didn't mean to tell you all that stuff about my football scholarship and the knee injury, but it's kind of funny, you start talking even when no one but a machine is listening, you open up. Strangely . . . about things that you don't talk about. I don't tell people that story. I don't know why. I think maybe it would just be too hard for people to believe that that used to be my life 'cause I'm so different now. I don't know. But I don't tell people that. But I told you, Ishmael. So I figure I probably won't hear this one online, but you did say you listen to them all. So I hope that this one was enjoyable for you. Bye. ☎

Playing for Pizza by John Grisham..........................4616
The Art of Fielding by Chad Harbach.......................1006
The Art of Learning by Josh Waitzkin.......................2833
The Boys in the Boat by Daniel James Brown..........3844
The Maze Runner by James Dashner.......................6881
The Power of One by Bryce Courtenay.....................1043
Us Against You by Fredrik Backman........................2943

Strangers

A Christmas Carol by Charles Dickens 1019
A Tree Grows in Brooklyn by Betty Smith 8629
Let the Great World Spin by Colum McCann 9501
Pride and Prejudice by Jane Austen 4632
The People Look Like Flowers at Last by Charles Bukowski 7334
The Stranger by Albert Camus 4626
The Stranger by Albert Camus 7917

Strength

I Am Malala by Malala Yousafzai 8888
I Know Why the Caged Bird Sings by Maya Angelou 8737

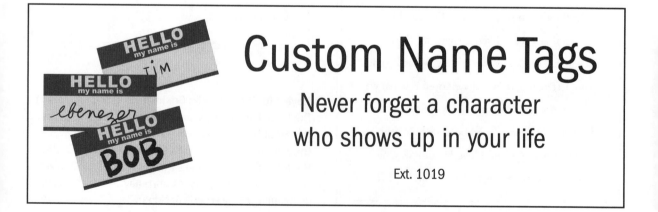

 To hear any of these stories, dial 774-325-0503 and dial the four-digit extension.

An anonymous voicemail message about

I Am Malala by Malala Yousafzai

Ext. 8888

Hi, Ishmael. I'm here to talk about *I Am Malala* by Malala Yousafzai. As soon as I got it I started reading it, 'cause I'd heard a lot about her, that she was fighting for rights in Pakistan or India and she had been attacked for it. So I started reading it and it made me think about something that happened to me once. I was going to a job interview, so I was dressed nicely. It was kind of a windy day out, and I was walking downtown. I live in a state where there are a lot of kinds of hicks or rednecks around, and I was waiting to cross the street and a big pickup truck full of guys in camo slowed down to the corner and leaned out and asked me how much I charged. I flipped them off and walked away, but it just made me so angry. Just for a minute, I had forgotten that I live in a world in which a lot of girls are objectified in that way and aren't given the rights that they should have. Especially Malala. She was attacked in a much more severe way than a lot of people—certainly more than I was. But there are still women in first world countries who are attacked and abused. It's a real thing. I think that a lot of people just refuse to acknowledge it. I really, really admire Malala for standing up and being a symbol for peaceful fighting, which I really relate to. I've always been the peacemaker struggling with how to fight for what I believe in but not come across as a pushover. I think that she's really equipped me with ways that I can stand up for myself, and for my beliefs in a really strong way without being violent or being aggressive. I definitely aspire to be like her. So thank you so much. This is a really good idea, and props for it. And have a good day. Bye. ☎

Recovering from Reality by Alexis Haines................7676
The Diary of a Young Girl by Anne Frank..................4850

Students

A Thousand Acres by Jane Smiley 2113
Brown Bear, Brown Bear, What Do You See?
by Bill Martin Jr. 9829

Tattoos

Teachers

Text us your pictures of great literary ink.

We'll feature bookish tattoos online @callingishmael.

_774-325-0503_

An anonymous voicemail message about

The Bell Jar by Sylvia Plath

Ext. 4465

Hey. My name's Kelly. In tenth grade I read a book called *The Bell Jar*. Sylvia Plath's writing, just everything she talks about, it's very confessional writing, which I've always enjoyed. And I've kind of developed my own writing off of her books, especially this one. A chapter that resonated a lot was when she's swimming out to sea and she's listening to her heart beat and she just keeps saying over and over again, "I am. I am." I thought that that was extremely powerful, to say words are similar to our heartbeats. My sophomore year of college, I was going through a really rough time and not doing too well and kind of was giving up on life a little bit. After spending a night drunk, crying in my shower, and really just wanting to end my life, the next day I woke up and got the words "I am" tattooed right below my heart. And now things are a little bit better. Maybe not every day, but slowly, you know, you listen to your heart beat. And you count your heartbeats. And you hope that one day you never lose count. So far I'm still counting. And that's my story. ☎

An anonymous voicemail message about

The Catcher in the Rye by J. D. Salinger

Ext. 6969

Hi, my name is Debbie and I want to talk about *The Catcher in the Rye*. The first time I read *Catcher*, I was in high school and my teacher Mrs. Schott was very enthusiastic about it. She was really excited that we were going to read it, and she told us it was how teenagers really are. I was interested because she was so enthusiastic about it, but of course I felt absolutely no connection to it whatsoever. I thought it was kind of pointless. And then I read it again two or three years later, when I was eighteen or nineteen and I was in college, and I liked it a little more. What struck me at that time was Holden's mental breakdown. How he keeps looking for help but he can't find anyone to trust and he keeps getting worse and worse. I loved that the book is this journey from the beginning, when he first gets kicked out of school, until his absolute breakdown. I really appreciated that. I read it again when I was in my twenties and I had moved to New York City, and that was cool, 'cause I understood the setting of the book a little bit more. I realized that one of my brothers was just like Holden. He was so arrogant and so negative all the time and too cool for anything and so difficult—and I realized for the first time that Holden is not likable in a lot of ways and it wouldn't be really fun to be around him or to be his parent. In my thirties I was an ELA teacher and I thought about Mrs. Schott's enthusiasm when she had introduced the book to us, so I tried to be just as enthusiastic so I could try to hook my students. I had lost a brother at that point, and this time I really connected to Holden's grief and his pain and his loss. I realized how much of the book is about that—about just his grief, and how he hasn't processed the loss of his sibling. I don't think there's really enough written about that topic of sibling loss. Now I'm a parent, and I don't know if it happened when I was pregnant or when my son was first born, but I remember realizing at one point that I understand the title in a completely different way. That I connect now to Holden and his tenderness and his instinct. That he just wants to protect the vulnerable people. He wants to protect children. I connect to that, and I think about how much we need catchers in the rye, and wouldn't it be nice if we could have one with everything that's going on in the world? So that's my story. Thank you for doing this project, and thank you for listening. Bye. ☎

On Such a Full Sea by Chang-Rae Lee 5988
Playing for Pizza by John Grisham..........................4616
She's Come Undone by Wally Lamb 1813
The Art Spirit by Robert Henri 2356
The Catcher in the Rye by J. D. Salinger..................2841
The Catcher in the Rye by J. D. Salinger..................6969
The Giver by Lois Lowry 6860
The Grapes of Wrath by John Steinbeck 2361
The House on Mango Street by Sandra Cisneros.....6874
The Mozart Season by Virginia Euwer Wolff 7884
The Odyssey by Homer 7888
The Razor's Edge by W. Somerset Maugham...........8897
The Scarlet Letter by Nathaniel Hawthorne............9905

Technology

Little Brother by Cory Doctorow 5762
Wool by Hugh Howey...4604

Tennessee

Bloodroot by Amy Greene.......................................4961

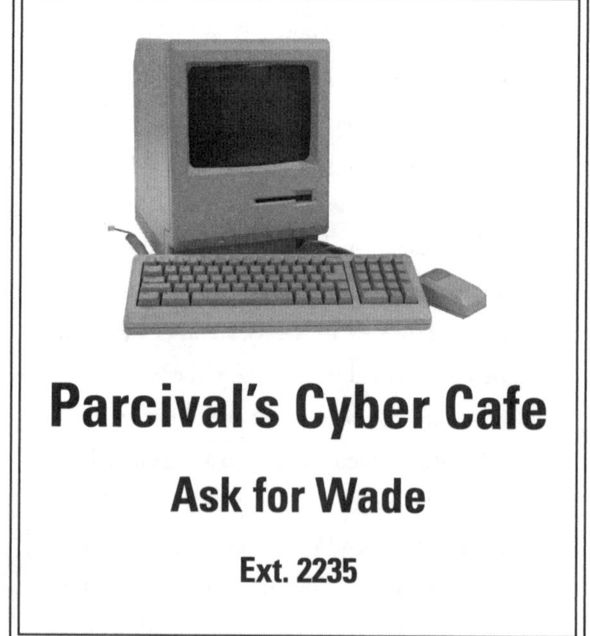

Parcival's Cyber Cafe

Ask for Wade

Ext. 2235

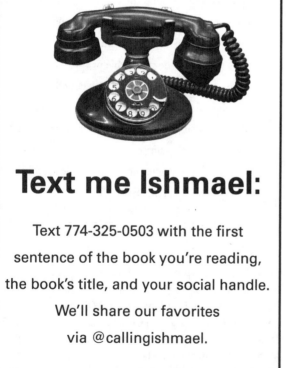

TENNESSEE BOOKSTORES

- ❑ A Little Bookish: Ooltewah
- ❑ Big Elephant Books: Chattanooga
- ❑ Bound Booksellers: Franklin
- ❑ Bubba's Book Swap: Kingsport
- ❑ Burke's Book Store: Memphis
- ❑ Dog Moon Books: Oliver Springs
- ❑ Duck River Books: Columbia
- ❑ Hudabam Booksellers: Clarksville
- ❑ I Love Books Bookstore: Kingsport
- ❑ Landmark Booksellers: Franklin
- ❑ McKay's Used Books: Chattanooga, Knoxville, Nashville
- ❑ Mr. K's Used Books, Music and More: Johnson City
- ❑ Novel.: Memphis
- ❑ Parnassus Books: Nashville
- ❑ Reading Rock Books: Dickson
- ❑ Southland Books and Cafe: Maryville
- ❑ Star Line Books: Chattanooga
- ❑ The Bookshop: Nashville
- ❑ The Rabbit Room: Nashville
- ❑ The Sewanee Bookstore: Sewanee
- ❑ Union Ave Books: Knoxville

INTERVIEWS WITH TENNESSEE BOOKSTORES

Ext. 6658

Listen to stories from some of our favorite bookshops in Tennessee.

Alex Haley Museum and Interpretive Center

Ext. 9031

200 Church Street
Henning, TN 38041

Texas

INTERVIEWS WITH TEXAS BOOKSTORES

Ext. 5966

Listen to stories from some of our favorite bookshops in Texas.

Bennu Coffee

Ext. 9843

515 S. Congress Ave.
Austin, TX 78704

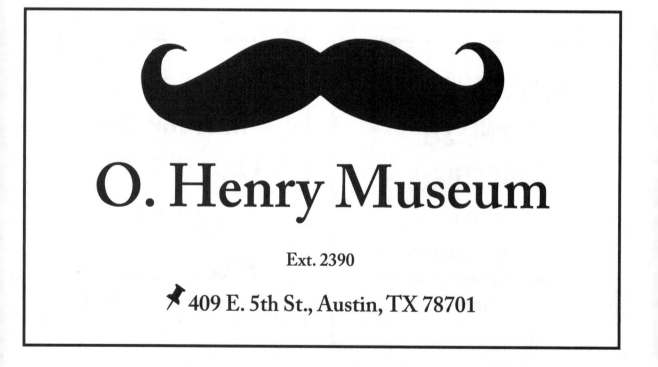

O. Henry Museum

Ext. 2390

409 E. 5th St., Austin, TX 78701

TEXAS BOOKSTORES

- ❑ A New Chapter: Greenville
- ❑ Absolutely Fiction Books: Lufkin
- ❑ AndEllaM Co.: Richardson
- ❑ Arts & Letters Bookstore: Granbury
- ❑ Barron's of Texas: Longview
- ❑ Baylor Bookstore: Waco
- ❑ Bibliobar: Garland
- ❑ Big Bend Natural History Association Park Store: Terlingua
- ❑ Black Pearl Books: Austin
- ❑ Black World Books: Killeen
- ❑ Blue Willow Bookshop: Houston
- ❑ Body Mind & Soul: Houston
- ❑ Bookmarc's: La Porte
- ❑ BookPeople: Austin
- ❑ BookWoman: Austin
- ❑ Brazos Bookstore: Houston
- ❑ Burrowing Owl Books: Canyon
- ❑ By the Book Bookstore: Corpus Christi
- ❑ Copperfield's Books: Spring
- ❑ Cowboy Bookworm: Fort Worth
- ❑ Deep Vellum Books: Dallas
- ❑ Enda's Booktique: Duncanville
- ❑ Fabled Bookshop & Cafe: Waco
- ❑ Fleur Fine Books: Port Neches
- ❑ Front Street Books: Alpine
- ❑ Gladewater Books: Gladewater
- ❑ Glow Worm New & Used Books: Spring
- ❑ Half Price Books: Arlington, Austin, Beord, Burleson, Cedar Park, College Station, Corpus Christi, Dallas, Fort Worth, Frisco, Garland, Houston, Humble, Kirkwood, Irving, Lewisville, Mansfield, McKinney, Mesquite, Pearland, Plano, Richardson, Rockwall, Round Rock, San Antonio, San Marcos, Sugar Land, Tyler, Watauga
- ❑ Indie Lector: Austin
- ❑ Interabang Books: Dallas
- ❑ Katy Budget Books: Houston
- ❑ Kinokuniya: Austin, Carrollton, Plano
- ❑ Lark & Owl Booksellers: Georgetown
- ❑ Magnolia Market: Waco
- ❑ Malvern Books: Austin
- ❑ Monkey and Dog Books: Fort Worth
- ❑ Muddy Water Bookstore: Navasota
- ❑ Murder by the Book: Houston
- ❑ Next Wave Books: Carrollton
- ❑ Noteworthy: Stamford
- ❑ Old Main Bookstore: Palacios
- ❑ Old Town Books: San Angelo
- ❑ Pan-African Connection Bookstore: Dallas
- ❑ Paragraphs on Padre Boulevard: South Padre Island
- ❑ Patchouli Joe's Books & Indulgences: Leander
- ❑ Play on the Strand: Galveston
- ❑ Pretty Things & Cool Stuff: Dallas
- ❑ River Oaks Bookstore: Houston
- ❑ Sententia Vera Cultural Hub Bookshop: Dripping Springs
- ❑ South Congress Books: Austin
- ❑ Texas Star Trading Co.: Abilene
- ❑ Texian Books: Victoria
- ❑ The Book Haus: New Braunfels
- ❑ The Book Nook: Brenham
- ❑ The Bookworm Box: Sulphur Springs
- ❑ The Dock Bookshop: Fort Worth
- ❑ The Lift: Houston
- ❑ The Published Page Bookshop: Cleburne
- ❑ The Storybook Garden: Weslaco
- ❑ The Twig Book Shop: San Antonio
- ❑ The Wild Detectives: Dallas
- ❑ Wide Open Books: Houston

Time

An anonymous voicemail message about

The God of Small Things by Arundhati Roy

Ext. 6862

All right, so I'm calling to talk about a book I love, *The God of Small Things* by Arundhati Roy. What I love about this book, and the reason it has so much meaning to me, is that it illustrates to me the amazing power of words—specifically how you can read the same words more than once but get a different meaning each time you read. The first time I read *The God of Small Things* I was probably in middle school, maybe in my early high school years. Needless to say, I missed a lot of what was happening. What I did not miss, however, was the beautiful language Roy uses. I remember being drawn to the words in that book in a way I hadn't been before, yet I know I didn't understand it at the time. I remember my parents being a little shocked that I read the book and that I liked it. I think they were pretty certain that I didn't take much out of it. The next time I read it, I was in college and this time I picked up on so much more of the narrative. I caught much of the anguish and tragedy that I missed the first time. I reread it again a couple of years ago, and stumbled across nuances in the narrative that I had missed in my previous reads. I found myself walking away with yet another impression of the book. Each time I read it, I was enraptured by the language, which to my mind is unlike any other novel I've ever read. Each time I read it, I feel like I'm reading a different story. That's what I love so much about the book—not necessarily the actual book, which on its own is incredible, but the experience. *The God of Small Things* illustrates the ways in which we go through our lives encountering events, people, and challenges that we have experienced at different times in our lives before. But the way we respond to these events and people and challenges, it changes with a new perspective that we gain as we age. You know how the summer vacation home that you visited every year as a child looked awfully different in your twenties and then again in your thirties and your forties? That person you couldn't stand in college who is a lot more bearable when you realize that it was your own hang-ups and insecurities that stood in the way of the friendship? The scenes look different when the frame changes. I can't wait for my fourth read of *The God of Small Things* because there's surely more to be discovered. So thank you, Ishmael. ☎

WATCH REPAIR

A few dozen hours can affect the outcome of a whole lifetime.

Call: 6862

The Immortalists by Chloe Benjamin 6876
The Oldest Living Things in the World by Rachel Sussman 7563
The Time Traveler's Wife by Audrey Niffenegger......1044

Transitions

Of Human Bondage by W. Somerset Maugham 1668
Oh, the Places You'll Go! by Dr. Seuss.....................9824
Serious Pig by John Thorne....................................1114
Severance by Ling Ma..1811
The Razor's Edge by W. Somerset Maugham...........8897
Watership Down by Richard Adams 9834

Travel

13 Little Blue Envelopes by Maureen Johnson 3355
A Little Life by Hanya Yanagihara............................2643
Anna Karenina by Leo Tolstoy 4659
Arabian Sands by Wilfred Thesiger 4660
Cat's Cradle by Kurt Vonnegut 5677
First They Killed My Father by Loung Ung................9712
Jonathan Livingston Seagull by Richard Bach 1218
Leaving the Atocha Station by Ben Lerner...............5757
Michael Collins and the Troubles by Ulick O'Connor..7815
Tales of a Female Nomad by Rita Golden Gelman....2832

THE OVERLOOK

OUR SHINING REPUTATION PRECEDES US!

Reserve your room today: 9374

Roaming with Rita Luggage Co.

Travel-tested in: Mexico, Borneo, the Galápagos Islands, and beyond

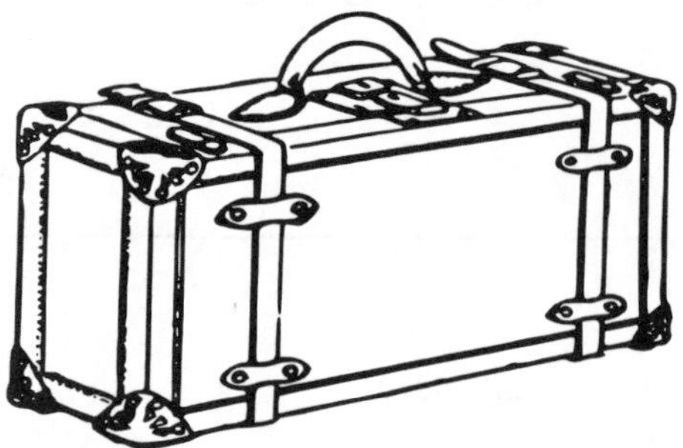

Carry on today! 2832

VACANCY

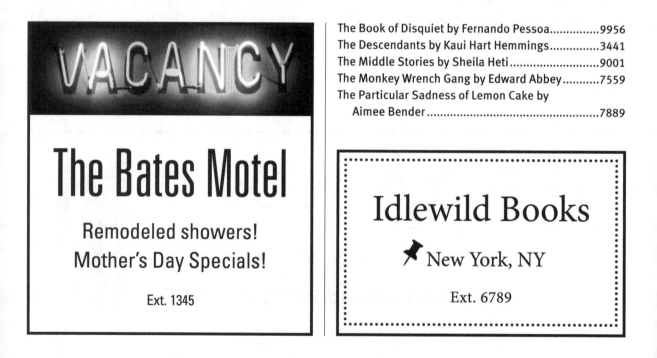

The Bates Motel

Remodeled showers!
Mother's Day Specials!

Ext. 1345

The Book of Disquiet by Fernando Pessoa 9956
The Descendants by Kaui Hart Hemmings 3441
The Middle Stories by Sheila Heti 9001
The Monkey Wrench Gang by Edward Abbey 7559
The Particular Sadness of Lemon Cake by Aimee Bender 7889

Idlewild Books

Ext. 6789

Under/Overrated

Fifty Shades of Grey by E. L. James..........................6804
Friday Black by Nana Kwame Adjei-Brenyah 8400
Homestuck series by Andrew Hussie 9822
I Am the Messenger by Markus Zusak......................8735
Moby-Dick by Herman Melville................................1010
Pedro Páramo by Juan Rulfo...................................2802
To Kill a Mockingbird by Harper Lee........................5813
Twilight by Stephenie Meyer 6668

Undercover

Harriet the Spy by Louise Fitzhugh 8725
Matilda by Roald Dahl 5002
The Velveteen Rabbit by Margery Williams..............6920

Utah

The Monkey Wrench Gang by Edward Abbey...........7559
Under the Banner of Heaven by Jon Krakauer..........1493

INTERVIEWS WITH UTAH BOOKSTORES

Ext. 2203

Listen to stories from some of our favorite bookshops in Utah.

CALL ABOUT A BOOK YOU READ UNDER THE COVERS WITH A FLASHLIGHT: 774-325-0503

HEAR WHAT OTHER BIBLIOPHILES SAY: 8044

ARCHES NATIONAL MONUMENT

Ext. 1844

Arches National Park Moab, Utah 84532

UTAH BOOKSTORES

- ❑ Atticus Coffee & Teahouse: Park City
- ❑ Back of Beyond Books: Moab
- ❑ Dolly's Bookstore: Park City
- ❑ Marissa's Books & Gifts: Salt Lake City
- ❑ Pioneer Book: Provo
- ❑ The Book Bungalow: St. George
- ❑ The Book Garden: Bountiful
- ❑ The King's English Bookshop: Salt Lake City
- ❑ The Peregrine House: South Jordan
- ❑ The Printed Garden: Sandy
- ❑ Weller Book Works: Salt Lake City

Vermont

She's Come Undone by Wally Lamb 1813
The Secret History by Donna Tartt 9768

INTERVIEWS WITH VERMONT BOOKSTORES

Ext. 5020

Listen to stories from some of our favorite bookshops in Vermont.

Robert Frost Interpretive Trail

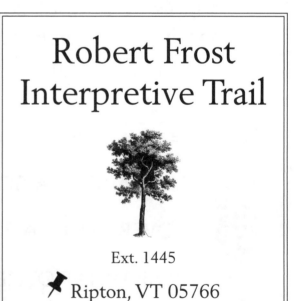

Ext. 1445

Ripton, VT 05766

VERMONT BOOKSTORES

- ❑ Bartleby's Books: Wilmington
- ❑ Bear Pond Books: Montpelier, Stowe
- ❑ Blair Books & More: Chester
- ❑ Boxcar & Caboose: St. Johnsbury
- ❑ Bridgeside Books: Waterbury
- ❑ Crow Bookshop: Burlington
- ❑ Ebenezer Books: Johnson
- ❑ Everyone's Books: Brattleboro
- ❑ Green Mountain Books: Lyndonville
- ❑ Next Chapter Bookstore: Barre
- ❑ Northshire Bookstore: Manchester Center
- ❑ Norwich Bookstore: Norwich
- ❑ Phoenix Books: Burlington, Essex Junction, Rutland
- ❑ Star Cat Books: Bradford
- ❑ The Bennington Bookshop: Bennington
- ❑ The Book Nook: Ludlow
- ❑ The Bookstore: Brandon
- ❑ The Eloquent Page: St. Albans
- ❑ The Flying Pig Bookstore: Shelburne
- ❑ The Galaxy Bookshop: Hardwick
- ❑ The Literary: Morrisville
- ❑ The Vermont Book Shop: Middlebury
- ❑ The Yankee Bookshop: Woodstock
- ❑ Village Square Booksellers: Bellows Falls

Virginia

Bridge to Terabithia by Katherine Paterson............4959
House of Leaves by Mark Z. Danielewski................4625
Pilgrim at Tinker Creek by Annie Dillard.................4605

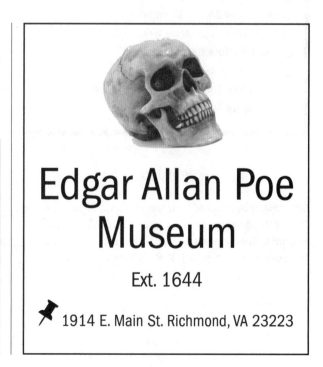

INTERVIEWS WITH VIRGINIA BOOKSTORES

Ext. 4982

Listen to stories from some of our favorite bookshops in Virginia.

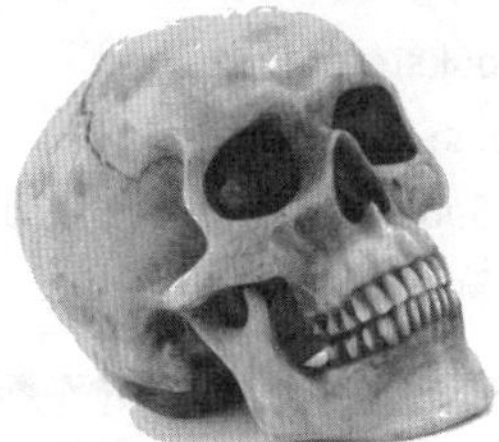

Edgar Allan Poe Museum

Ext. 1644

 1914 E. Main St. Richmond, VA 23223

VIRGINIA BOOKSTORES

- ❑ 2nd Act Books: Charlottesville
- ❑ AFK Books & Records: Virginia Beach
- ❑ Arte of the Booke: Roanoke
- ❑ Bards Alley: Vienna
- ❑ bbgb: Richmond
- ❑ Blue Moon Antique Mall and Bookstore: Lovingston
- ❑ Book No Further: Roanoke
- ❑ Book People: Richmond
- ❑ Books and Crannies: Martinsville
- ❑ Books and Other Found Things: Leesburg
- ❑ Books, Beads and More: Mechanicsville
- ❑ Books Bound2Please: Orange
- ❑ Busboys and Poets: Arlington
- ❑ Buteo Books: Arrington
- ❑ Chapters Bookshop: Galax
- ❑ Child's Play!: Arlington, McLean
- ❑ Chop Suey Books: Richmond
- ❑ Flights of Imagination: Williamsburg
- ❑ Fountain Bookstore: Richmond
- ❑ Givens Books: Lynchburg
- ❑ Harambee Books & Artworks: Alexandria
- ❑ Hooray for Books!: Alexandria
- ❑ New Dominion Bookshop: Charlottesville
- ❑ Old Town Books: Alexandria
- ❑ One More Page Books: Arlington
- ❑ Over the Moon Bookstore & Artisan Gallery: Crozet
- ❑ Peach Street Books: Cape Charles
- ❑ Prince Books: Norfolk
- ❑ Pufferbellies Toys & Books: Staunton
- ❑ Read Early and Daily: Arlington
- ❑ Reston's Used Book Shop: Reston
- ❑ Sacred Circle: Alexandria
- ❑ Scrawl Books: Reston
- ❑ Stories Like Me: Fairfax
- ❑ Sundial Books: Chincoteague
- ❑ Tales of the Lonesome Pine: Big Stone Gap
- ❑ The Book Bin: Onley
- ❑ The Book Dragon: Staunton
- ❑ The Little Bookshop: Midlothian
- ❑ The Open Book: Warrenton
- ❑ The Up Center: Norfolk
- ❑ The Virginia Shop: Richmond
- ❑ Winchester Book Gallery: Winchester

Walking

On Looking by Alexandra Horowitz 4599
On the Road by Jack Kerouac 3795
Pilgrim at Tinker Creek by Annie Dillard 4605
The Lord of the Rings by J. R. R. Tolkien...................7811

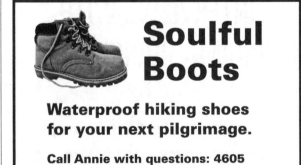

Where the Sidewalk Ends Bookstore

Chatham, MA

Ext. 7880

Wanderlust

Around the World with Auntie Mame by Patrick Dennis....................4628
Atlas of World History edited by Patrick K. O'Brien ...1030
Moby-Dick by Herman Melville....................4776
On the Road by Jack Kerouac 3795
Quest for the Lost City by Dana and Ginger Lamb ...2800
The Alchemist by Paulo Coelho....................2362

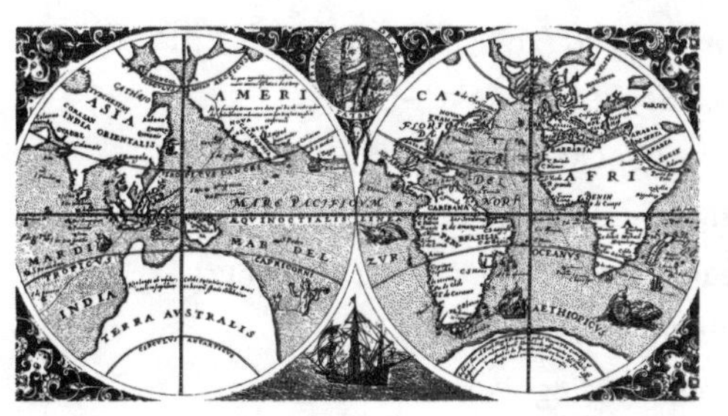

Moriarty's Maps

Zigzag coast to coast . . .
You can't beat our routes!

Call Jack: 3795

Washington

The Art of Racing in the Rain by Garth Stein............7204
The Boys in the Boat by Daniel James Brown 3844
Twilight by Stephenie Meyer 6668

INTERVIEWS WITH WASHINGTON BOOKSTORES

Ext. 9098

Listen to stories from some of our favorite bookshops in Washington.

The Brautigan Library

Ext. 7654

1511 Main St., Vancouver, WA 98660

Miller Tree Inn

BED AND BREAKFAST

Ext. 7646

654 E. Division St., Forks, WA 98331

WASHINGTON BOOKSTORES

- ❑ . . . and BOOKS, too!: Clarkston
- ❑ 2nd Look Books: Spokane
- ❑ 3rd Street Book Exchange: Marysville
- ❑ A Book for All Seasons: Leavenworth
- ❑ A Good Book: Sumner
- ❑ A Novel Bookstore: Yelm
- ❑ Ada's Technical Books and Café: Seattle
- ❑ Adventures Underground: Richland
- ❑ Arundel Books: Seattle
- ❑ Auntie's Bookstore: Spokane
- ❑ Away with Words Bookshop: Poulsbo
- ❑ Ballast Book Co.: Bremerton
- ❑ Book & Game Company: Walla Walla
- ❑ Book Larder: Seatlle
- ❑ Book 'N' Brush: Chehalis
- ❑ Brick & Mortar Books: Redmond
- ❑ Browsers Bookshop: Olympia
- ❑ Captain's Nautical Supplies: Seattle
- ❑ Couth Buzzard Books: Seattle
- ❑ Darvill's Bookstore: Eastsound
- ❑ Dickens Children's Books: Vancouver
- ❑ Eagle Harbour Book Co.: Bainbridge Island
- ❑ Earthlight Books: Walla Walla
- ❑ East West Bookshop: Seattle
- ❑ Edmonds Bookshop: Edmonds
- ❑ Elliott Bay Book Company: Seattle
- ❑ Griffin Bay Bookstore: Friday Harbor
- ❑ Half Price Books: Bellevue, Everett, Lynnwood, Redmond, Tacoma, Tukwila
- ❑ Henderson Books: Bellingham
- ❑ Horizon Books: Seattle
- ❑ Inklings Bookshop: Yakima
- ❑ Island Books: Mercer Island
- ❑ Jerrol's: Ellensburg
- ❑ King's Books: Tacoma
- ❑ Kingfisher Bookstore: Coupeville
- ❑ Kingston Bookery: Kingston
- ❑ Kinokuniya: Seattle
- ❑ Last Word Books: Olympia
- ❑ Left Bank Books: Seattle
- ❑ Liberty Bay Books: Bremerton, Poulsbo
- ❑ Lopez Bookshop: Lopez Island
- ❑ Madison Books: Seattle
- ❑ Magnolia's Bookstore: Seattle
- ❑ Main Street Books: Monroe
- ❑ Mercer Street Books: Seattle
- ❑ Moonraker Books: Langley
- ❑ North Bank Books: Stevenson
- ❑ Odyssey Books & Gifts: Port Angeles
- ❑ Open Books: A Poem Emporium: Seattle
- ❑ Orca Books: Olympia
- ❑ Page 2 Books: Burien
- ❑ Paper Boat Booksellers: Seattle
- ❑ Pearl Street Books & Gifts: Ellensburg
- ❑ Phinney Books: Seattle
- ❑ Phoenix Rising: Port Townsend
- ❑ Port Book and News: Port Angeles
- ❑ Queen Anne Book Company: Seattle
- ❑ Riverwalk Books: Chelan
- ❑ Secret Garden Books: Seattle
- ❑ Teaching Toys and Books: Tacoma
- ❑ Teaching Toys, Too: Gig Harbor

WASHINGTON BOOKSTORES (CONT.)

- ❑ The Bookery: Ephrata
- ❑ The Globe Bookstore: Seattle
- ❑ The Neverending Bookshop: Edmonds
- ❑ The Sequel Books: Enumclaw
- ❑ The Traveler: Bainbridge Island
- ❑ Third Place Books: Burien, Lake Forest Park, Seattle
- ❑ Three Trees Books: Burien
- ❑ Time Enough Books: Ilwaco
- ❑ Trail's End Bookstore: Winthrop
- ❑ Uppercase Bookshop: Snohomish
- ❑ Vashon Island Books: Vashon
- ❑ Vault Books & Brew: Castle Rock
- ❑ Village Books: Bellingham, Lynden
- ❑ Vintage Books: Vancouver
- ❑ Watermark Book Company: Anacortes
- ❑ Wind and Tide Bookshop: Oak Harbor
- ❑ Wishing Tree Books: Spokane
- ❑ Writers' Workshoppe & Imprint Books: Port Townsend

Washington, DC

American Wife by Curtis Sittenfeld 7562
Dust Tracks on a Road by Zora Neale Hurston 7694
Open Windows by Joel Church 2797
Sing, Unburied, Sing by Jesmyn Ward......................3941

National Museum of African American History and Culture

1400 Constitution Ave. NW
Washington, DC 20560

Ext. 5217

Library of Congress

Ext. 1645

101 Independence Ave. SE, Washington, DC 20540

INTERVIEWS WITH WASHINGTON, DC, BOOKSTORES

Ext. 3424

Listen to stories from some of our favorite bookshops in Washington, DC.

WASHINGTON, DC, BOOKSTORES

- ❑ Big Planet Comics
- ❑ Bridge Street Books
- ❑ Busboys and Poets: 14th & V, Anacostia, Brookland, Takoma
- ❑ Child's Play!
- ❑ Duende District Bookstore
- ❑ East City Bookshop
- ❑ Fairy Godmother
- ❑ Kramerbooks & Afterwards
- ❑ Lost City Bookstore
- ❑ Loyalty Bookstore
- ❑ MahoganyBooks
- ❑ Middle East Books and More
- ❑ Politics and Prose: Northwest DC, The Wharf, Union Market
- ❑ Potter's House Books
- ❑ Reiter's Books
- ❑ Sankofa Video Books and Café
- ❑ Solid State Books
- ❑ Tempo Bookstore
- ❑ Wall of Books

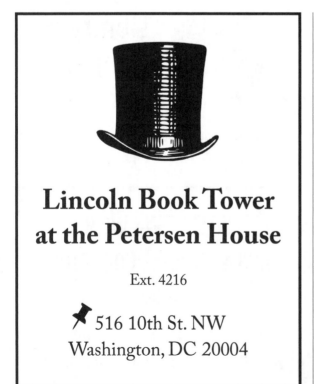

Lincoln Book Tower at the Petersen House

Ext. 4216

516 10th St. NW
Washington, DC 20004

West Virginia

Shiloh by Phyllis Reynolds Naylor............................6496
The Glass Castle by Jeannette Walls.........................3493

INTERVIEWS WITH WEST VIRGINIA BOOKSTORES

Ext. 5316

Listen to stories from some of our favorite bookshops in West Virginia.

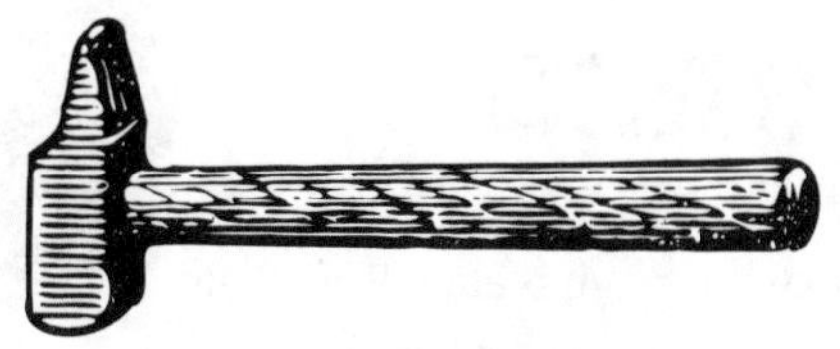

John Henry Statue

Ext. 1625

Hwy. 12, Talcott, WV

WEST VIRGINIA BOOKSTORES

- ❑ A New Chapter: Lewisburg
- ❑ Four Seasons Books: Shepherdstown
- ❑ Taylor Books: Charleston
- ❑ The Inner Geek: Huntington

Wisconsin

American Gods by Neil Gaiman 3655
American Gods by Neil Gaiman 4656
American Wife by Curtis Sittenfeld 7562
Blankets by Craig Thompson 3018
Evicted by Matthew Desmond 9707
Little House on the Prairie series by Laura Ingalls Wilder 5759
The Art of Fielding by Chad Harbach 1006

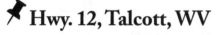

INTERVIEWS WITH WISCONSIN BOOKSTORES

Ext. 8978

Listen to stories from some of our favorite bookshops in Wisconsin.

House on the Rock

Ext. 1118

5754 WI-23
Spring Green, WI 53588

WISCONSIN BOOKSTORES

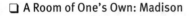

- ❑ A Room of One's Own: Madison
- ❑ Apostle Island Booksellers: Bayfield
- ❑ Arcadia Books: Spring Green
- ❑ BayShore Books: Oconto
- ❑ Blue House Books: Kenosha
- ❑ Book Heads: Plymouth
- ❑ Book Stop: Green Bay
- ❑ Bookends on Main: Menomonie
- ❑ Books & Company: Oconomowoc
- ❑ Boswell Book Company: Milwaukee
- ❑ Chapter2Books: Hudson
- ❑ Chequamegon Book & Coffee Company: Washburn
- ❑ Daily Books: Mazomanie
- ❑ Dotters Books: Eau Claire
- ❑ Dragonwings Bookstore: Waupaca
- ❑ Driftless Books & Music: Viroqua
- ❑ Fair Isle Books: Washington Island
- ❑ Half Price Books: Appleton, Brookfield, East Madison, Greenfield, West Madison
- ❑ Honest Dog Books: Bayfield
- ❑ InkLink Books: East Troy
- ❑ Liddle Bee Books: Sparta
- ❑ Lion's Mouth Bookstore: Green Bay
- ❑ Literatus & Co.: Watertown
- ❑ Mind Chimes Bookshop: Three Lakes
- ❑ Mystery to Me: Madison
- ❑ Northwind Book & Fiber: Spooner
- ❑ Novel Bay Booksellers: Sturgeon Bay
- ❑ Porchlight Book Company: Milwaukee
- ❑ Redbery Books: Cable
- ❑ River Dog Book Co.: Beaver Dam
- ❑ The Little Read Book: Wauwatosa
- ❑ Thomas A. Lyons Fine Books: Neenah
- ❑ Travelin' Storyseller: River Falls
- ❑ Yardstick Books: Algoma

Wisdom

Brave New World by Aldous Huxley........................5673
Figuring by Maria Popova........................9711
Franny and Zooey by J. D. Salinger........................4608
I Wrote This for You by Iain S. Thomas........................8736
Inherit the Wind by Jerome Lawrence and Robert E. Lee........................9327
Old School by Tobias Wolff........................1979
Song of the Lioness quartet by Tamora Pierce........................1818
The Diary of a Young Girl by Anne Frank........................4850
The Oldest Living Things in the World by Rachel Sussman........................7563

Writers/Writing

Ariel by Sylvia Plath........................4661
Eragon by Christopher Paolini........................4602
Fear and Loathing in Las Vegas by Hunter S. Thompson........................9709
I Am the Messenger by Markus Zusak........................3842
If You Want to Write by Brenda Ueland........................7741
My Name Is Asher Lev by Chaim Potok........................3682
Old School by Tobias Wolff........................1979
On the Road by Jack Kerouac........................5495
Tales of a Fourth Grade Nothing by Judy Bloom........................8013

An anonymous voicemail message about

The Oldest Living Things in the World by Rachel Sussman

Ext. 7563

Hi, Ishmael. I have a problem with forgetting. Some days I feel like there's so many things fighting for my attention, cutting it up into pieces, dividing it and dividing it again until there's nothing left. The world moves so quickly today. New experiences are always just a click away. That's changed the world for the better, but I'm worried that we don't take enough time to stop and be present and experience those moments. To sit with them and make them part of our past. Instead, we just let them pass. It's like we need to protest against forgetting. That's what Rachel Sussman's *The Oldest Living Things in the World* does for me. When I see a photo of a thirteen-thousand-year-old tree and read its story, it's like I'm tapping into deep time and my tiny life gets to experience something so big. That tree carries its whole history inside in every ring. I feel like her book is telling me to slow down and take time to remember because every lifetime is just a moment to that tree, but in every moment we can find a lifetime. Thanks. ☎

An anonymous voicemail message about

Tales of a Fourth Grade Nothing by Judy Blume

Ext. 8013

When I was a kid, I had a hard time learning how to read. So my grandmother came up with the idea of reading together. I would read the book to her. The first book I picked was *Tales of a Fourth Grade Nothing* by Judy Blume. It took about a week to read together and then afterwards she asked me what I thought. And I told her that I liked the book but I would have done it differently. So we made our own stories about those characters and their adventures. It became a tradition to read together and to make up our own stories afterwards. Years later, I still love to write and read and make my own stories. And I think a large part of that is reading as a kid with my grandmother. So thank you, Grandma. ☎

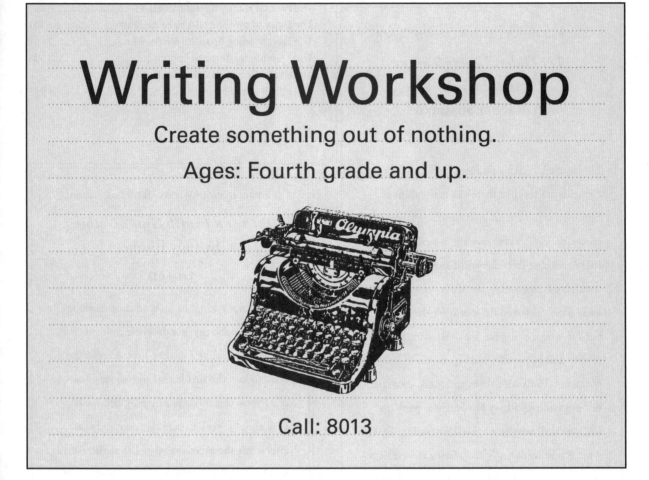

Writing Workshop

Create something out of nothing.

Ages: Fourth grade and up.

Call: 8013

Write in Books, People Who

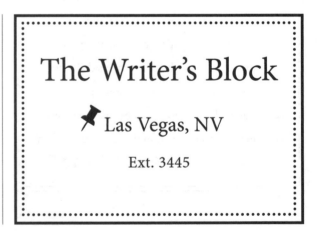

The Writer's Block

Las Vegas, NV

Ext. 3445

 To hear any of these stories, dial 774-325-0503 and dial the four-digit extension.

BOOKS TO CALL ISHMAEL ABOUT:

The first book you remember reading: ______________.

The best book you've ever received as a gift: ______________.

The book you read at exactly the right time: ______________.

An anonymous voicemail message about

To Kill a Mockingbird by Harper Lee

Ext. 1964

I have a first edition of *To Kill a Mockingbird* at home. It was first published in 1960. When I was in sixth grade—way too young to be reading this novel—I obviously had no respect for first editions. There are smiley faces and inked-in hearts all over the endpapers. But you know, here it is, battered by my childish graffiti. It's got strings coming out of the binding. It's messed up. But fifty-five years later, it's still here and it's survived. And that's saying something. I've read this novel four times. Each time I'm freshly struck by its perfectness. Perhaps the greatest compliment to a novel is its ability to survive the test of time—to be reread so often, right? I mean, I'm a reader. I really am an active reader, but I don't think I've ever read any other novel four times. Here's the thing: *To Kill A Mockingbird* reads aloud incredibly well. I know this because the last three times I've read it aloud to each of my three oldest children, and each time the same thing happens. The kid listens, becoming enraptured by Scout and Jem and Dill and their antics with Boo Radley, but deep, deep into this novel, during one of the courtroom scenes, each of these three children has an identical response, which is this: Once it's been revealed that Tom Robinson has had his left arm mangled in a mill machinery accident, they are immediately relieved. It's now clear to them that Tom couldn't possibly be guilty. *Finally*, they think. *The wheels of justice will be turning.* This is always the saddest moment for me as a reader. I keep reading and I watch the confusion and just plain disbelief on their young faces each time as they discover that sometimes the truth is simply not a defense. I think that given recent racially driven horrors, this remains so powerfully poignant to me, this book. To witness the purity and innocence of children as they move shockingly into the grip of reality. It just stuns me each time. I have one more child to read this novel aloud to. And perhaps he'll surprise me. But I doubt it. And certainly I'll never tire of Harper Lee's world. That's it. Thanks, Ishmael. ☎

Wyoming

WYOMING BOOKSTORES

- ❑ Jackson Hole Book Trader: Jackson
- ❑ Legends Bookstore: Cody
- ❑ Sheridan Stationery Books and Gallery: Sheridan
- ❑ Storyteller: Thermopolis
- ❑ The Second Story: Laramie
- ❑ Valley Bookstore: Jackson
- ❑ Whistle-Stop Mercantile: Douglas
- ❑ Wilson Book Gallery: Wilson
- ❑ Wind City Books: Casper

INTERVIEWS WITH WYOMING BOOKSTORES

Ext. 9395

Listen to stories from some of our favorite bookshops in Wyoming.

Historic Occidental Hotel

Ext. 1119

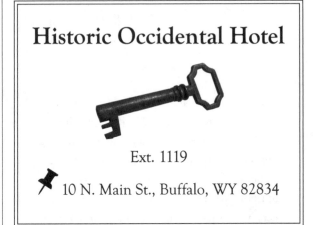

 10 N. Main St., Buffalo, WY 82834

CALLS

by

BOOK TITLE

#

A

B

 To hear any of these stories, dial 774-325-0503 and dial the four-digit extension.

C

D

E

F

G

H

I

J

K

L

M

N

O

P

Q

R

S

T

U

W

Y

Z

CALLS

by

AUTHOR

A

B

C

D

E

F

G

H

I

J

K

L

M

Q

R

S

T

U

V

W

Y

Z

ACKNOWLEDGMENTS

Anonymous Callers 5021

Julianna Haubner 1255

Jofie Ferrari-Adler, Ben Loehnen, Lauren Wein, Meredith Vilarello, Jordan Rodman, Alison Forner, Alexandra Primiani, Morgan Hoit, Amanda Mulholland, Brigid Black, Jessica Chin, Paul Dippolito, and the entire team at Avid Reader Press 8801

Lucy Carson, Molly Friedrich, and Heather Carr....................2121

Sam Johnson and Mo Mohamed 2200

Dan Kedmey, Thaniya Keerepart, Lisa LaBracio, Andrew Lloyd-Jones, Jai Punjabi, Aaron Rasmussen, Nick Waldrip, Gerta Xhelo, and Kirill Yeretsky 7222

Negar Saei, Amanda Filingeri, Jackie Goldstein, Jenna Wohlwend, and Nathan Horne 1431

Julia Barrett 6711

Hannah Epstein 3449

Paul, Tim, Terrie, Barbara, Jill, Emma, Ben, Annie, Lucy, Lainey, and Taco 2199

Booksellers, librarians, teachers, and readers 4394

ABOUT THE AUTHORS

Stephanie Kent is a writer and multimedia producer. Her recent work includes the Webby Award–winning *Masters of Scale* podcast, the *Wall Street Journal*'s premiere mobile-first news app, and a series of book reviews for *Boxing Insider*. During her time on staff at TED, Steph built community programs and brand engagement strategies. She was awarded a 2017 Creative Community Fellowship with National Arts Strategies Foundation and holds a BA in playwriting and literature from Emerson College. Stephanie writes a weekly newsletter on creativity, and is a competitive boxer. You can find her online at stephkent.com.

Logan Smalley is the founding director of TED's award-winning youth and education initiative, TED-Ed, which creates and distributes free educational animations and programs to students and teachers around the world. Prior to working for TED, Logan was selected as a TED Fellow for his roles as director, editor, and composer in the acclaimed, feature-length documentary, *Darius Goes West.* Logan began his career as a high school special education teacher in his hometown of Athens, GA, and holds a masters degree in technology, innovation, and education from the Harvard Graduate School of Education. You can learn more about Logan and his work at logansmalley.com.